DIVIDED

8 PARTITIONS THAT
CHANGED THE WORLD

AGASTYA MITTAL

INDIA · SINGAPORE · MALAYSIA

ISBN

Hardcase 979-8-89446-347-6
Paperback 979-8-89415-266-0

Contents

Preface

A partition is defined by Merriam-Webster Dictionary as "the action of parting: the state of being parted: DIVISION." This division can be physical, like a fence put up between my house and that of my neighbor; it can be political, like the creation of different states in the US out of one chunk of territory; or it can be geographical, like a river or mountain range that creates a natural divide. In geopolitics, a partition usually refers to the separation of a territory or people due to social or political reasons. Partitions are historically how most modern nation-states have been created. For example, the modern nation of Russia was created by the collapse of the Soviet Union in 1991, a situation that will be observed later in this book.

Partitions have been a prevalent theme in global history for millennia and have shaped every nation on Earth today in some way. Partitions don't just physically separate people but also create different societies, ecosystems, and cultures. A very early example of partition was that of the Carolingian Empire, a post-Roman kingdom in Western

Europe. Also known as Francia or the Frankish Empire, the vast realm was most famously ruled by Emperor Charlemagne. However, the land was carved up between his three grandsons, being split into West, East, and Middle Francia. Middle Francia was quickly absorbed into its two neighbors to the west and east, and eventually, West and East Francia evolved into two different states. In 987, West Francia came under the rule of the Capetian Dynasty, becoming the Kingdom of France, and then the nation of France as we all know it. East Francia, on the other hand, was renamed the Kingdom of Germany and expanded to conquer Italy, Burgundy, and other territories to the East. It was reorganized into the Holy Roman Empire, from which modern Germany traces its roots (along with multiple other nations).

While France and Germany have many similarities and lots of shared history, the two nations have completely different languages, cultures, foods, and systems of government. The German language derives from the language of Europe's Germanic tribes and kingdoms, while French is a Romance language, or a descendant of Latin, spoken by the Romans. This is a clear example of the profound impact the partition of the Carolingian Empire had on both peoples. The territories once held by Charlemagne would never again be completely united under a single regime until Napoleon's conquests of Europe in the 1800s, nearly 1,000 years after the initial divide of the Frankish realm. Although in today's world, Germany and France are close allies and both members of NATO and the EU, historically, both have been at odds with one another frequently. The two sides directly warred in the Napoleonic Wars, the Franco-Prussian War, World War I, and World War II, to name only a few relatively recent examples. It's possible that, had the Carolingian Empire never been split, the entire land encompassing France, Germany, and its neighbors that either directly or indirectly owe their borders to those two nations would've been united under one banner, one culture and one lifestyle.

Another example of a partition that created modern nation-states is that of the New World, a region modernly known as the Americas. When the continent's existence was revealed to Europe, it wasn't long before European powers like Spain, Portugal, the Netherlands, France, and England began establishing colonies and spheres of influence. Portugal and Spain, for instance, signed the Treaty of Tordesillas, an agreement that, with the input of the Pope, split the Americas (particularly South America) between the two nations. The Portuguese claim was later adjusted, and the territory gained independence a few hundred years later and became the modern nation of Brazil, which shares many aspects of Portuguese culture, including Portuguese language, cuisines, and religion. The Spanish side of South America became the modern nation-states of Argentina, Chile, Peru, Bolivia, Paraguay, Uruguay, Venezuela, Colombia, and Ecuador. All of these nations speak the Spanish language, eat foods that are inspired by Spanish food, and retain many aspects of Spanish culture, including Catholicism, the majority religion of Spain.

It's clear that partitions have been responsible for the creation of the Earth's ~200 nations today. The bifurcation of one people into two has been the reason every major ethnicity and grouping of people on Earth exists. The Latin-speaking Romans became the people of France, Italy, Spain, Portugal, Romania, and other nations. They spoke those nations' namesake languages, as well as smaller languages and dialects like Occitan, Catalan, and Sardinian. The Medieval Turkic people of Central Asia (a group with unclear origins) are responsible for the existence of a wide array of Turkic peoples today, including Turks (of Turkey), Uzbeks, Kazakhs, Uyghurs, and nearly forty other ethnic groups ranging in membership from a few hundred to tens of millions of people.

Whatever the reason, whether it be the creation of a barrier or the natural evolution of a group of people in two different sets of circumstances, partitions have caused innumerable social, political, and economic effects around the globe, and they have completely shifted how humans act today as a species and as a civilization. The following chapters will lay out eight of the most impactful partitions of the modern era, how they came about, and what happened as a result of them.

01

Africa – A Continent of Untold Stories

The partition of Africa is unique in that it's not just about a country or region but an entire continent. Infamously, the continent was partitioned between the European great powers into colonies and spheres of influence, with large swathes of the continent being divided into new, artificially created territories. Unfortunately, the effects of this partition were almost entirely negative for Africans, with the lines drawn arbitrarily dividing nations, peoples, and territories and lumping together new groups of people.

Even worse than this was the European exploitation of the African continent. They harvested resources, enslaved the local people, and destroyed or destabilized hundreds of societies across the land. The effects of these partitions were seen almost immediately following decolonization and even to this day. So how did such a dreadful partition come about, and how was it allowed?

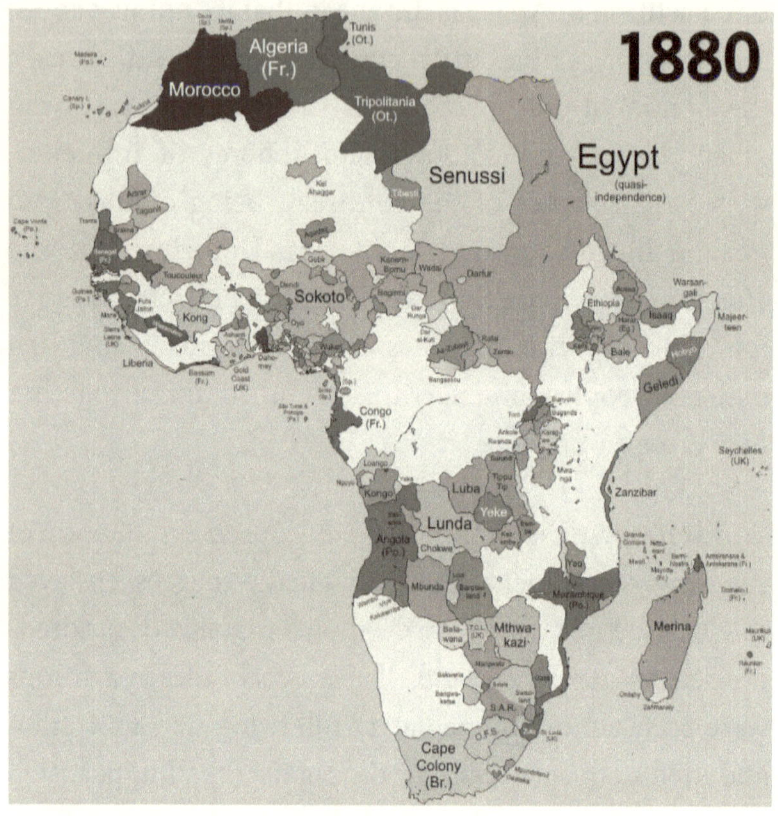

Above: Africa in 1880, before the full extent of European colonization

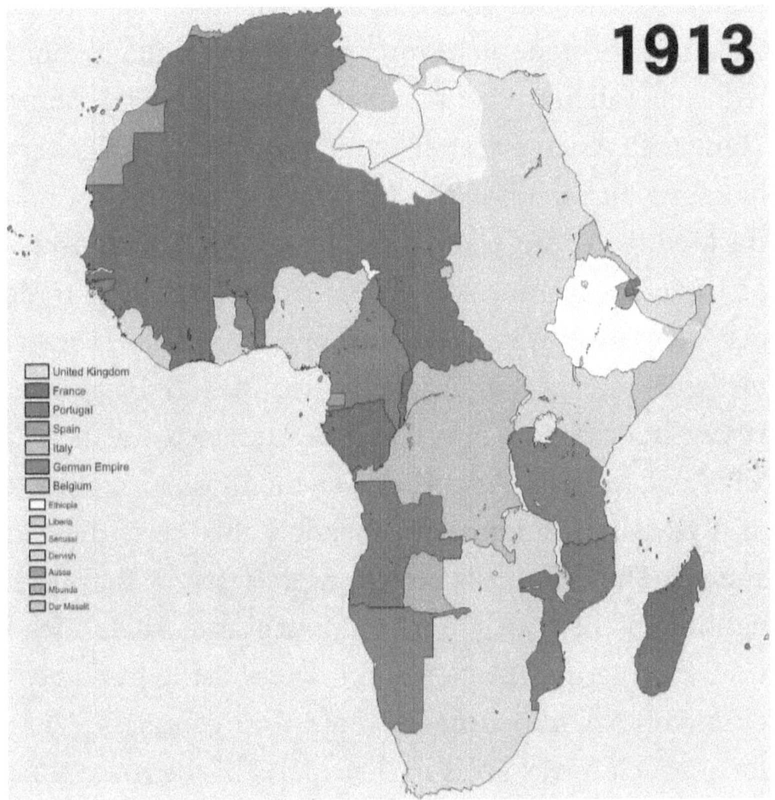

Africa in 1913, when most of the continent had been divided

Africa was a land known to Europeans for more than 5,000 years. Since thousands of years before Christ, civilizations on both continents traded and interacted with each other, starting with trade between Ancient Egypt and the Minoans in modern-day Crete, Greece. Religions like Christianity, Islam, and Judaism were present in both Africa and Europe. For centuries afterward, Europe continued to have both friendly and hostile encounters with the North African Saharan regions of the Ottoman Empire, such as Egypt and the Sudan. The modern history of European interactions with Sub-Saharan Africa actually starts in the 15th century. Trade with Asian places, like India and China, was a very lucrative business for the European great powers, and the Mediterranean Sea was usually regarded as the center of trade and commerce, particularly concerning trade between Europe and Asia. European ships would travel to the Byzantine Empire-controlled Middle East, from where trade expeditions could be launched via the old Silk Road routes to Asia. However, the Ottoman conquest of Byzantium completely upended this centuries-old system. The Ottomans already were wary of European nations in their neighborhood, such as Portugal, who tried closing the Red Sea and monopolizing trade near Ottoman Arabia in the 15th and 16th centuries. They forced such heavy taxes in their parts of the routes that they fell completely into disuse. This meant Europeans needed a new way to reach Asia.

Starting with Portuguese explorer Bartolomeu Dias in 1488, Europeans started going around the Southern tip of Africa to reach Asia (some others tried going around the world and ended up in the New World, which will be important momentarily). These nations began to establish trading posts and colonies in Africa. Portugal was the first nation to establish a foothold in the African continent, forging relations with Kingdoms on Africa's

West Coast, like Kongo, Ndongo, and Matamba, these three being located in present-day Angola, DR Congo, Republic of the Congo, and Gabon. It wasn't long, though, before Portugal began to get involved in the local politics and happenings in the region.

The great power began to see great value in Africa. The people there would be relatively easy for Portugal to subjugate, and it would give the Portuguese a place to harvest resources such as gold. In addition, Portugal could spread Christianity to Kongo and other kingdoms in the region, as well as use the region for potential explorations of inner Africa. One especially big draw for Portugal was Africa's potential as a supplier for their other ventures, like in India and the East Indies.

As mentioned previously, many European nations had launched expeditions to circumnavigate the globe, ending up in what is now called the Americas. It didn't take too much time before they discovered the immense resources available to harvest in the New World, resulting in a scramble to establish colonies and spheres of influence in the Americas. Spain got the lion's share, taking modern Mexico, a large portion of the Western United States, Central America, more than half of South America, and lots of Caribbean colonies. France gained a colony known as New France that included a large chunk of Eastern North America. Portugal was no different. In the 1494

Treaty of Tordesillas, Pope Julius II drew a line on a map that split the unclaimed world between Spain and Portugal, the two first nations to reach the New World. Most of Portugal's share fell under what is now Brazil. Brazil was a highly lucrative colony for the Portuguese. Cash crops like sugarcane and coffee grew richly there, aided by the warm, wet climate.

To run such a colony, a great deal of manpower was necessary to ensure maximum production. Unfortunately, Portugal decided to use slavery in their colonies to boost efficiency. As Portugal took heightened interest in local politics and wars, they offered to supply the local states with weaponry and support in exchange for trade rights and slaves, among other things. Initially, this arrangement worked for both Portugal and the African kingdoms, but the former intentionally ramped up conflicts. Rumors started among European nations that precious metals and materials, such as gold, silver, and ivory, were available in Africa's interior. Portugal used their base of operations in Luanda to sell more goods to local rulers and gain more slaves, while societies ripped themselves apart and European control ever-strengthened. The Portuguese made their way to Mutapa, a kingdom in modern-day Zimbabwe and Mozambique, amid rumors of a great silver mine. So Portugal, through some initial explorations of coastal Africa, eventually gained ownership of two massive colonies in Southern Africa, Angola, and Mozambique, as well as other smaller territories like Guinea-Bissau and Madeira.

Another situation is observed in South Africa. In 1652, the Netherlands set up a fort near the Cape of Good Hope, the southernmost tip of the African continent. This fort later grew into Cape Town (Dutch: *Kaapstad*) and became the capital of the Dutch Cape Colony. Unlike Portugal, where the European nation established subsidiary alliances with African nations and asserted control through these vassals, the Dutch ran their colony directly. The ethnic makeup of Dutch South Africa was greatly changed by the drastic influx of Dutch and French Huguenot settlers into the colony, who came to be known as Boers or Afrikaners. The Dutch and their descendants conflicted with the native peoples, particularly the Khoisan, who were ethnically cleansed and scattered across South Africa following a rebellion. Many of the European settlers and their descendants were farmers, and they moved beyond Cape Colony's borders into inner South Africa, setting up Boer Republics like the Orange Free State and South African (Transvaal) Republic.

During the Napoleonic Wars, the British Empire annexed Cape Colony from the Dutch. They also took surrounding areas such as Zululand by feuding with the local people. Thousands of British settlers flocked to the Boer Republics but were denied civil rights and liberties by the Afrikaners. Britain demanded reforms from the republics, but in vain. Thus, they fought wars with the Orange Free State and Transvaal, eventually annexing both republics into Cape Colony and creating the Union of South Africa. This was to be an independent nation in union with the British Crown, similar to Australia, Canada, or New Zealand. Unfortunately, there were significant tensions between the different racial groups in the multiethnic South Africa. This multiracialism is evidenced by the fact that South Africa today has eleven official languages: the indigenous Zulu, Xhosa, Northern Sotho, Tswana, Sotho, Tsonga, Venda, Swazi, and Southern Ndebele languages; Afrikaans (the language of those of Dutch descent); and English. The different languages, by and large, correspond to South Africa's different ethnic groups, and all of these ethnicities were lumped together, which caused issues. The White minority, mostly descendants of the British or Dutch, ran the government and instituted racial policies against the Black majority that were codified as *apartheid* in 1948. This system completely stripped Blacks of their rights and subjected them to violence and lower-class treatment. They had to carry IDs with them when visiting places that weren't reserved for them, for example, and this system didn't end until the early 1990s.

From just the two examples of Portuguese colonies and South Africa, we can understand exactly what Europeans looked for in African colonies and what happened as a result of these colonies' creation. The European colonizers sought resources such as gold and diamonds, they sought labor to work their plants, and they sought to remove or assimilate indigenous peoples. As a result of these policies, African societies were destroyed in many instances, divided in many others, and colonized/subjugated in all. Perhaps the single event that best exemplified the division of Africa happened in 1884 and 1885.

By the late 1800s, most European great powers had become well-established in Africa. The British, French, Portuguese, and Germans controlled large swathes of the continent, with smaller shares belonging to the Italians, Ottomans, and Spanish. However, there were still several problems that required mitigation. For one, territorial disputes were present between multiple nations. The Horn of Africa, a region in the continent's East, was under claims by France, Italy, and the UK. As a result, German Chancellor Otto von Bismarck called the Berlin Conference in 1884, meant to represent all European great powers with a stake in the continent (and the United States). Each nation presented its claims, and depending on previous ownership, overlapping claims, the balance of power, and the relative power each nation held at the time, borders were drawn. The British had established themselves in Egypt some years before and were eyeing the Sudan, nominally an Ottoman province. They also controlled Uganda and Kenya, as well as Southern African territories all the way up to Northern Rhodesia (today Zambia). As the most powerful European nation, they wanted and demanded a complete, contiguous British line of colonies running from Egypt in the North to South Africa in the South. The French, for their part, already had a good foothold in Africa before the conference. They had trading ports in Senegal and had seized both Algeria and Tunisia in 1830 and 1881, respectively. They also had made headway into inner West Africa, including Mali, Niger, and Mauritania. They wanted most of West Africa under their control. The rest of the nations represented either didn't have the strength or existing claims that Britain or France had, so they weren't entitled to the same colonies. Italy, Portugal, Germany, and Spain gained multiple smaller colonies.

Importantly, a region in Central Africa known as the Congo Free State (today's Democratic Republic of the Congo) was contested by each nation due to its vast resources (particularly rubber), waterways, and connectivity to other regions in Africa. The region was awarded to King Leopold II of Belgium, who was a third party whose country was small and politically neutral. The Congo was to be open to trade for all nations, even nations like Russia, Austria-Hungary, or the US, which had no possessions in Africa. The exact boundaries of the Congo were divided with no regard for the people living in the region, dividing peoples and societies. Areas that were extremely lucrative and contested were added to the territory, such as Katanga, a region in the Congo's extreme southeast with swampy marshlands and lots of big game for hunting. If one looks at a map, one can see that most of the modern DR Congo has borders that are either straight lines or that fall on rivers, geographic boundaries that have little correlation with ethnic divides. Leopold also treated the Congo with such brutality and malice that the rest of Europe's great powers, such as Britain and France, who were not well-respected for their own treatment of colonies, internationally condemned his actions. In Congo's rubber plantations, slaves would be mutilated, maimed, and killed if they failed to meet their strenuous

Left: "This image depicts a native Congo man with rubber coils tangled around his body. At the top of the coils is the head of King Leopold II, oppressing the man. This image shows what life was like during imperialism and its negative effects. King Leopold would enslave the Congolese to go farm rubber latex. They would often work very long hours, and when taking off the rubber, it would harm their bodies and skin. [M]any of the workers were shot if they didn't fill the quota." - Braithwaite

rubber quotas. The Belgian government took control of Congo from Leopold in 1908.

The ensuing colonization of the continent split peoples permanently and changed entire cultures. Nigeria is one example of a nation with various contrasting peoples lumped together due to geography or convenience. The Hausa people of West Africa were split by the Niger-Nigeria border, with the two colonies being controlled by France and the UK, respectively. Nigeria has two distinct parts: a Muslim North and a Christian South. The Muslim North is mostly Hausa and Fulani peoples who speak Chadic languages, a branch of Afroasiatic languages, a larger language family that also contains Arabic, Hebrew, Berber, and other vernaculars. The South is home to several ethnicities, including Igbo and Yoruba peoples. The grouping of ethnicities caused great tension when Nigeria declared independence, as the country was left to figure out its method of government. Unresolved tensions, such as Igbo nationalism, kicked off the Biafra War, in which Igbo-majority states declared independence as *Biafra*. Each of the nation's ethnicities tended to hold different roles in the new nation (Hausa generally made up most of the army, Igbo managed Nigeria's burgeoning oil industry, etc.) The ensuing civil war killed up to 100,000 combatants and 4,000,000 civilians due to mass famines, caused in part by the Nigerian government cutting off trade and supplies to Biafra, a region that was never given the resources to be agriculturally independent.

The partition of the African continent, which started centuries ago, continues to affect the continent in every way today. In 1977-78, during the height of the Cold War, Communist Somalia, ruled by military dictator Siad Barre, invaded its fellow Communist nation Ethiopia, whose Eastern region of Ogaden was populated mostly by ethnic Somalis. The resulting Ogaden War killed 25,000 people and displaced 500,000 more. Ethiopia's victory in the war resulted in the international isolation of Somalia, discontent within the army against the regime, and the eventual overthrow of Barre's government, followed by the complete collapse of the government and economy and a state of civil war and poverty since 1991 that continues to the present day.

Territorial disputes continue to exist across the continent, such as Egypt's border with Sudan and Morocco's claim on the Spanish exclaves of Ceuta and Melilla, which are located on the African mainland. Rebellions and wars plague the land, such as in Mali, whose Northern half is populated with Tuareg people who have intermittently fought for sovereignty before and since Mali's independence.

Of course, many areas in the continent are very successful, such as Tunisia, which threw off a dictatorship through the Arab Spring Protests in 2010 and has become a free, prosperous democracy since then. Botswana, one of Africa's few countries to have never been under the control of a dictatorship, has seen great levels of economic success, especially in recent decades. Mauritius, an island nation in the Indian Ocean, has the best quality of life on the continent, which is helped in part by its tourism industry. But in some places, a cycle of corruption, poverty, and disease has plagued Africa for decades and made it very difficult for the people there to progress and develop. Luckily, Africa as a whole is in a far better spot than it was when its nations won independence in the mid to late-20th century. Hopefully, Africa's existing problems will be solved soon, and the continent can be the prosperous center of knowledge and innovation it was often known as in antiquity.

02

Israel – Two States, One Territory

One of the most impactful redrawings of borders in the modern era is that of the Middle East. The region, situated at the crossroads of Asia, Africa, and Europe, is today considered a geopolitical hotbed and one of the most influential and important areas of the world economically, politically, and culturally. Encompassing Turkey, Iran, Iraq, Syria, Lebanon, Israel, Jordan, Kuwait, Saudi Arabia, Egypt, Cyprus, Yemen, Oman, Bahrain, Qatar, the United Arab Emirates, and the Palestinian Territories, the region is incredibly ethnically diverse. The Middle East is the site of some of the great cities of the ancient world, including Jerusalem, Damascus, and Baghdad. The region once included some of the world's first empires, like the Assyrians and Babylonians, and was the birthplace of the Abrahamic religions, three of the largest faiths on Earth: Judaism, Christianity, and Islam. Throughout its long and occasionally turbulent history, the Middle East has been divided among several empires, nations, and peoples.

The Middle East came under Islamic control with the foundation of the Rashidun Caliphate, which politically united the domains spiritually under the Prophet Muhammad's control. The ruler of this empire was known as the *Khalifa*, or Caliph, the spiritual successor to Muhammad. Subsequent caliphates were ruled by dynasties whose rulers would take this title, religiously and politically uniting the Sunni Islamic

Middle East. Since then, almost the entire Middle East has been Muslim. In the 1400s and 1500s, the Turkic Ottomans conquered Anatolia (in modern-day Turkey) and expanded into Mesopotamia, the Levant, and Hejaz, the latter of which contained the Holy cities of Mecca and Medina. This united much of the Middle East under Ottoman rule. The rest of the Middle East was controlled either by the Shi'ite Persians (today Iran) or smaller states on the Arabian peninsula, such as Oman or the Saudi Emirate of Diriyah.

The Ottomans would continue their vast conquests and expand into the Balkans and North Africa, reaching the pinnacle of their power in the mid-16th century. At this point, nearly the entire Middle East, excluding Persia, was controlled either directly or indirectly by the Ottoman Sultanate. They had conquered most of North Africa and some of East Africa, annexed the Caucasus region, and much of Southern Europe, going all the way from Greece to Hungary. They even besieged Vienna, the capital of the mighty Holy Roman Empire, in 1529, although this failed.

A few centuries later, however, cracks began to show in the Ottoman Empire's once-indestructible foundation. They began to lose their vassals and spheres of influence in various parts of Europe, such as Crimea, Georgia, and Hungary, which either declared independence or were conquered by a larger power like Russia. The 16th and 17th centuries also saw the Mediterranean lose its importance as a trade hub, with trading power shifting to the newly discovered Americas, to which the Ottomans had no access. Internal corruption and a second failed siege of Vienna drove the final nail in the coffin of Ottoman superpower status, and the once-powerful, mighty empire soon became known as the *Sick Man of Europe*.

The empire slowly crumbled through the 1700s and into the 1800s. By this point, the Ottomans only had direct control of its Middle Eastern territories, with North African states like Algiers, Tunis, and Tripolitania (now Algeria, Tunisia, and Libya) being run by hereditary regents who were independent in all but name. The Ottoman presence in the Balkans was slowly fading as well, with rebellions breaking out in many of the Sultanate's Christian-majority areas. European great powers smelled blood in the water and moved to assert their own presence, with Russia marching into the Caucasus and Austria moving into the Balkans. France annexed Algiers in 1830 and Tunis in 1881, while the United Kingdom took control of Egypt in 1882. Nations like Bulgaria, Greece, and Albania seceded, and Italy captured Tripolitania. By now, the Ottomans only controlled their core territory of Anatolia, Mesopotamia, the Levant, and the Hejaz.

In 1914, the Ottomans decided to stage a last-ditch attempt to regain some of their former glory and joined World War I on the side of the Central Powers with Germany, Austria-Hungary, and Bulgaria. They aimed to recapture some territories they lost to Britain and Russia, reestablishing themselves as a European great power. However, this is exactly what did not happen. Even before the war had started, Britain and France began laying out plans to carve up the Sultanate's territories between themselves. They promised the Ottoman capital of Constantinople (now Istanbul), which was the center of Eastern Orthodox Christianity, to the Russian Empire, and the three nations fought the Ottomans.

In the 1916 Sykes-Picot Agreement, France and the UK secretly drew the borders for their future colonies in the Middle East. Russia would get Constantinople and Eastern Anatolia, while France would gain Syria and Lebanon, leaving Britain with Palestine (Israel, the West Bank, and Gaza), Transjordan (Jordan), and Mesopotamia (Iraq). The borders drawn in the region were very arbitrary and did not reflect ethnic, linguistic, or religious divisions, creating resentment against colonial authorities and among the inhabitants themselves. That year, the UK also sponsored an Arab revolt against the Turkish Ottomans in these territories to rid them of Ottoman influence, promising the Arabs that they would be permitted to create a united Arab nation in the Middle East. In 1917, the United Kingdom made the Balfour Declaration, stating their approval and support for a Jewish national homeland in Palestine, which contributed to the already-complicated problems in the region.

Although the French and British had also coveted territories in Turkish Anatolia, the new Turkish independence movement headed by Mustafa Kemal Ataturk stopped any action. Russia had descended into civil war, leaving Constantinople and Eastern Anatolia to the new Republic of Turkey that replaced the Ottoman Caliphate. In the 1923 Treaty of Lausanne, France and Britain came away with the territories they had coveted in Mesopotamia and the Levant, while Hejaz was conquered by the Saud Dynasty. Any foreign claims to Turkish territories were relinquished. The League of Nations, the new multinational organization meant to maintain world peace, awarded mandates to Britain and France to govern their territories in the Middle East. Britain established monarchies in Iraq and Jordan, ruling Palestine as a dual homeland for Jews and Arabs. They also negotiated several borders between nations like Kuwait, imposing protectorates over these nations and effectively controlling the state of affairs in many of them. These border shifts were again arbitrary and fueled resentment, which created ongoing tensions.

Petroleum had been discovered in Persia in 1908, but it wasn't until World War II that the true value of the mysterious black substance was understood fully. Many of the Middle East's nations, like Saudi Arabia, Iran, and Iraq, contained vast reserves of oil, which were promptly exploited by the Western powers. Although nearly all Middle Eastern colonies won independence in the interwar period or the decades following World War II, they were left to govern themselves almost immediately while still being substantially economically controlled by the West. One particular example of ethnic tensions erupting was in Mandatory Palestine. Owing to the region's religious preeminence to Judaism, Jewish people flocked there in the millions following the Holocaust in Europe. Consequently, this caused already-simmering tensions between Jews and Muslims in the region to reach a boiling point.

In an attempt to arbitrate between the two groups, the United Nations, which was the successor to the League of Nations, proposed a partition of the territory between the two groups, with the majority going to the Jews as the State of Israel, and the rest going to the Arabs for an independent Palestine. Trying to disrupt this process, a coalition of seven Arab nations invaded the land. However, they were defeated by the Jewish Israeli government, which annexed 60% of the territory allotted to Palestine under the United Nations peace plan. The remaining territories were the Gaza Strip, centered around the city of Gaza, and the West Bank, centered around the Eastern half of Jerusalem. Israel began to depopulate Palestinian villages in the former Palestinian lands. Egypt placed Gaza under military occupation, while Jordan formally annexed the West Bank.

Map of Israel and the Palestinian Territories after the Six-Day War

Tensions continued to simmer. In 1956, Israel invaded Egypt during the Suez Crisis, along with France and Britain, in response to Egypt nationalizing the canal and closing the Straits of Tiran, a waterway passing through Egypt, to Israel, despite the straits being vital to Israeli shipping. While the conflict was a disaster for the French and British, Israel gained international recognition as a regional power and only further deepened Arab-Israeli hostilities. In 1967, Egyptian President Gamal Abdel Nasser once again closed the Straits of Tiran, mobilized Egyptian forces on the border with Israel, and announced the withdrawal of the United Nations' forces, who had been sent to monitor the situation. In response, Israel launched a surprise attack against Egypt, capturing Gaza and Egypt's Sinai Peninsula. When Syria and Jordan joined Egypt, Israel defeated them as well and occupied the West Bank and Syria's Golan Heights, additionally annexing East Jerusalem and declaring a united Jerusalem to be the capital of Israel. Israel also won the 1973 Yom Kippur War, in which the Arab nations launched a surprise attack on the namesake holiday. They proceeded to establish Jewish settlements in the West Bank and displace Palestinians further.

In the wake of the Second World War and the success of decolonization movements throughout the Middle East and beyond, various nationalist movements spread in the region. One such movement was Zionism, which called for the establishment of a Jewish homeland and inspired the Balfour Declaration, culminating in the establishment of Israel. Another prevalent ideology was that of Pan-Arabism, or the unification of all Arab peoples into a single state. Numerous variations existed, such as Michel Aflaq's Ba'athism or Gamal Abdel Nasser's Nasserism. The Arab nations thus founded the Arab League in 1945 and took a united opposition to Israel. However, Israel's victories, particularly in 1967, severely weakened the Arab nations and made Israel a technologically dominant superpower with American assistance. Israel also annexed East Jerusalem, the half of Jerusalem that served as the capital of the Palestinian territories, and officially shifted its capital from Tel Aviv to Jerusalem. This drew strong condemnation from much of the international community, including even the United States, who refused to shift their embassy from Tel Aviv to Jerusalem until 2017. Israel began occupying sections of the West Bank and Gaza and setting up settlements for Israelis. This has resulted in the continuation of hostilities between Israel and its neighbors.

From 1967, the region also saw a major increase in American and Soviet presence, although the region was not a Cold War flashpoint like Vietnam or Germany, for example. The United States chose to support Israel due to historical ties and trade relationships. The Soviets pursued economic ties with the Arab World due to their mutual distrust of the West and their support for Arab nations with socialist influences, like Syria and Iraq. However, there was no so-called "battle of capitalism vs. communism" in the Middle East, and the overarching conflict there became more of a war between Jews and Arabs and of Jews and Muslims as a whole. To this day, twenty-eight nations don't maintain relations with Israel, most of them Islamic. There are also several nations that historically did not recognize Israel but later did so, like Egypt, Jordan, or Morocco, after an agreement or compromise. This clearly demonstrates the enmity between both sides.

Tensions have continued to rise with the presence of more extreme elements in the region in recent years. While the Oslo Accords in 1994 officially provided a settlement between Israel and Palestine with the endorsement of a two-state solution (both countries got the territories allotted to them in 1967), the reality hasn't been so peachy. In 1987, the Sunni fundamentalist organization Hamas was established, gaining control of the Gaza Strip and rejecting the notion of a two-state solution altogether. Hamas has carried out numerous attacks against Israel, the most recent and most destructive being the rocket strikes and invasion of Israel that was carried out from Gaza in 2023. Israeli President Benjamin Netanyahu has begun a large-scale invasion and bombing campaign of the Gaza Strip, kickstarting a full-scale war.

This will no doubt have massive implications for the world for years to come and may threaten to completely upend the status quo that had been in place for decades. Indeed, these implications have already begun to rear their ugly heads. The Israel-Palestine conflict and the Arab-Israeli conflict as a whole have claimed more than 100,000 lives since Israel's inception. The constant Arab defeats at Israel's hands have seen the realignment of national borders, the de-legitimization of existing regimes, and major changes in governments and foreign policy in various nations, such as Syria, where the 1948 defeat was widely regarded as a national tragedy and culminated in a coup and ten regime changes in the following decade. The 1967 war saw the largest implications for not only Israeli territorial growth but for Israel's own status as a regional power and counter to Arab influence in the region. Israel gained the Golan Heights and the Sinai Peninsula (the latter relinquished in 1981) and occupied the West Bank and Gaza Strip. They became a major world power and united not only Arabs but most of the Islamic world against them. Organizations like Hamas, ISIS, and Hezbollah have committed to Israel's permanent defeat and potential destruction. Tensions have risen with the presence of nations like the US and Russia in the area, with the US, in particular, selling advanced weaponry to Israel for many years.

The division of the British Mandate of Palestine into the modern-day nations of Israel and Palestine has caused widespread territorial disputes, tensions, and suffering for millions of people. Without regard for the well-being and wishes of either the Jews or Arabs, the land was carved up. As a result of this division, the region has become a war zone and weapon testing ground, unfortunately catching millions in the crossfire.

Picture of devastation in Gaza following Israeli bombing campaigns in 2023

03

Iraq – Split Down the Middle

Israel is not the only Middle Eastern nation affected by events that occurred 100 years ago. Iraq is another nation whose entire modern history has been shaped by the policies of the British Empire during and after World War I. Then known as Mesopotamia, Iraq was divided by the Ottomans into three *vilayets* or provinces: Baghdad, Basra, and Mosul, named after the namesake cities. When the Ottoman Empire joined World War I, the British smelled an opportunity to gain the large territory, which was said to contain large oil supplies. During the British Mesopotamian Campaign of World War I, British troops entered the provinces and annexed them from the Ottomans, being awarded a mandate over them by the League of Nations. In 1921, the British installed the Hashemite dynasty, said to descend from the Prophet Muhammad directly, into power. But the religious significance of the Hashemites did not guarantee them political goodwill from the people or the army.

In the 1910s, just prior to the First World War, the European powers all hoped to expand their influences to the Ottoman Middle East to gain access to the vast oil reserves they believed were present there. Britain and Germany, the two main players, formed African and Eastern Concessions Ltd., a company meant to bring their Middle Eastern economic interests together, both for oil and for other ventures such as the planned

Berlin-Baghdad railway. The next year, the company was renamed to the Turkish Petroleum Company, and their purpose became to acquire concessions from the failing Ottoman Empire through some of their largest companies, including Germany's Deutsche Bank, and Britain's Royal Dutch Shell and National Bank of Turkey. The largest stakeholder in this new company was the British-owned Anglo-Persian Oil Company, which owned 50% of the stock. The Turkish vizier agreed to the concessions on oil put forth, which gave the TPC a near-monopoly on oil in the region.

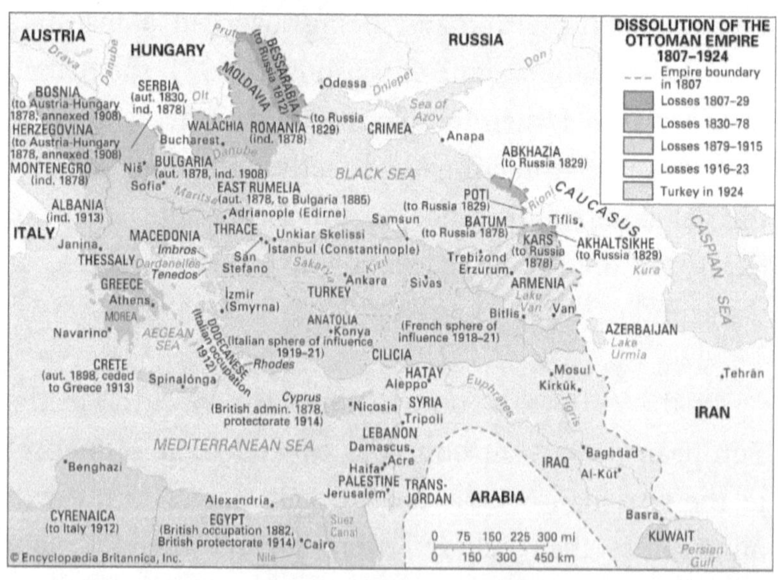

Map of the Ottoman Empire's territorial losses from the 1800s to 1924

After World War I, France inherited the defunct German Empire's stock. However, Britain's mandate over

Iraq granted them immense control over Iraqi foreign policy and economic policy, which didn't sit well with Iraqis. Even after Iraq's independence in 1932, they remained dependent on Britain for military and advisory aid, and British oil drilling in Iraq did not cease.

Following the Second World War, tensions were at an all-time high. Pan-Arabism, or the union of all Arab people into a single state, had become a widely espoused idea among the Iraqi populace, and part of this belief was the total removal of foreign agents like the British. Ideologies like Ba'athism and Nasserism, which advocated for anti-imperialism and Pan-Arabism, were widespread all across the Arab World. Egyptian President Gamal Abdel Nasser, who founded Nasserism, was the staunchest proponent of Pan-Arabism. Meanwhile, the Kingdom of Iraq continued to pursue ties with the British. While British oil companies were persuaded to give slightly higher commissions to the Iraqi government, most of this commission was to be set aside for industrial and infrastructure development, which would, in part, be overseen by European advisers. Spearheading this development initiative was a British economist, Sir James Arthur Salter. In 1948, Prime Minister Salih Jabr negotiated the Portsmouth Treaty with the British, which would see their military withdrawal from the country in exchange for British control over Iraqi military training, planning, and foreign affairs until 1973. Rebellions were launched in numerous parts of the country, but all were calmed down. In 1955, Iraq entered the Baghdad Pact, a defense agreement between the UK, Iran, Pakistan, and Turkey, which angered Arabs of all nations. Egypt, seeing this as a challenge to their own regional influence, took steps to remove the West from the region. They nationalized the Suez Canal, which prompted an invasion from Britain, France, and Israel. Iraq officially supported the British despite Egypt being an Arab nation. In 1958, when Egypt established the United Arab Republic as a confederation between them, Syria, and, to a certain extent, Yemen. Iraq elected not to join the union. Instead, they created the Arab Federation with their fellow Hashemite Kingdom of Jordan. However, this was viewed with mistrust and was considered a weak attempt to emulate the UAR.

Hashemite rule ended in 1958 when King Faisal II was overthrown and executed in a coup d'état headed by a group known as the Free Officers, led by Abd-al Karim Qasim, an army brigadier who declared Iraq a republic and assumed leadership. Supposedly a Pan-Arabist movement, the Free Officers purged the entire royal family and withdrew Iraq from both the Arab Federation and the Baghdad Pact. Qasim had forged strong ties with the Iraqi Communists, who were backed by the Soviet Union, which did not want Iraq to unify with the UAR. This caused significant tensions with the

Pan-Arab Nasserists and Ba'athis, as well as the rest of the Arab World, Iran, Turkey, and the West. Ironically enough, Qasim himself was overthrown in 1963 by the Iraqi Ba'ath Party, who were subsequently purged by the Nasserists.

During this time period, significant disputes had arisen between Iraq and some neighbors, particularly Iran, over the division of traditional lands between both nations dating back to the Ottoman-Safavid Wars from the 16th to 19th centuries. For example, Persian Iran had gained the Arab-majority Khuzestan, which was confirmed by the British. The large region of Kurdistan, inhabited by the Kurdish people, had been divided between the two powers for centuries and had fought for self-rule on many occasions. The British promised them a homeland in the Sykes-Picot agreement, but this promise was left unfulfilled. Since then, Kurds in both Iraq and Iran had launched low-scale rebellions against their respective governments. Even though neither nation wished to see an independent Kurdistan established, both sponsored rebellions in the other's territory.

The creation of Iraq as a single political unit by the British also had religious consequences. Iraq, being at the crossroads between Shi'ite Islamic Iran and the Sunni Arab World, had significant populations of both denominations. The nation was unique in that it was Arab-majority, but most of these Arabs were Shia Muslims, not Sunnis like the vast majority of Arabs in other nations. But while Shi'ites were the majority, the Sunni population still made up about a third of the nation and much of the political and social elite. This is why when Iran underwent an Islamic Revolution that saw its monarchy overthrown and replaced with a Shia Islamic clergy headed by Ruhollah Khomeini, the Ba'athist regime, now headed by Saddam Hussein, saw the new government as a threat to Iraq. Iraq believed that the revolution would cause sectarian issues within the nation to explode, especially as Khomeini actively advocated for the revolution to be exported to other nations. The tensions between the two nations culminated in a full-scale war in 1980 when Saddam invaded Iran. The ensuing war saw the deaths of millions of people and large-scale atrocities such as chemical warfare and the use of children as soldiers.

In 1991, Iraq invaded Kuwait under the accusation of slant drilling or the belief that Kuwait's oil drills near Iraq's border were slanted into Iraqi territory and stealing Iraqi oil. However, there were also several other reasons for the hostilities. Iraq had accrued a $14 billion debt with Kuwait fighting Iran, and Kuwait also refused to decrease shipments of oil, cutting global prices and putting a strain on Iraq's oil-dependent economy.

One more reason behind the invasion was Kuwait's creation as a whole. Kuwait, which was under the rule of semi-autonomous sheikhs since the 16th century, was legally a part of the Ottoman Empire until 1913, when Britain made it a protectorate, arbitrarily negotiated its borders, and separated it from the Arab-inhabited parts of the Ottoman Empire. Many Iraqis considered Kuwait to be culturally a part of Iraq, and this sentiment, plus the overarching Ba'ath ideology that still resonated in Iraq, gave Iraq cause to wage war against the small nation. Saddam invaded Kuwait and annexed it into Iraq, but a coalition of forty-two countries headed by the United States successfully defeated Iraq and liberated Kuwait in less than a year.

The hostility between Iraq and the US carried over into the 2000s when the United States used the September 11th attacks as a pretext to invade Iraq and overthrow the Ba'ath regime. Saddam was executed, and a massive power vacuum opened up. The nation thus fell into instability and insurgency. Various armed groups, including Hezbollah and scattered Ba'ath loyalists, began to openly wage war against each other. The most notorious and infamous of these groups was al-Qaeda in Iraq, an offshoot of al-Qaeda, the terrorist organization that perpetrated the September 11th attacks. This group eventually morphed into the Islamic State, a radical terror outfit that perpetrated mass killings of minorities like

Jews, Christians, Yazidis, and others that they deemed to be non-believers. They claimed to be a worldwide caliphate with control over all Muslims, although most Muslims rejected this.

US Army Sergeant fighting in Iraq during the Iraq War (2003-2011)

Even today, Iraq is plagued by instability and warfare that can be traced back to its very creation. The arbitrary creation of borders, the rule of unpopular governments, and the rise of dictatorships meant that the nation continues to experience difficulties to this day. Today, the nation's GDP per capita ranks 114th out of nearly 200 nations, and it places 7th on the Global Terrorism Index, which isn't helped by the fact that Iraq's government is notoriously corrupt and unable to combat terror threats on a large-scale. Unfortunately, the diverse, culturally significant nation has not seen much improvement since the British governed the land, and even today, it accepts large amounts of foreign aid. Of course, nothing would be better for Iraq than peace, but barring the creation of a stable and strong government, it will be difficult in the years ahead.

04

Ireland – A Walled Island

The partition of Ireland didn't directly impact the entire world so much as one particular region, but its effects have had an impact on much of the world. The island of Ireland, in the British Isles, is a very interesting case of a partition that affected the lives of everyone living there and continues to do so to this day. The history of Ireland is inextricably linked to that of Great Britain, including England, Wales, and Scotland. Britain has greatly shaped Ireland's destiny and future, including its current borders. The independent nation of Ireland controls most of the island, but a sizable portion is Northern Ireland, one of the four central British territories along with England, Scotland, and Wales. So how did Ireland, whose history as a culture and island goes back centuries, get partitioned?

To understand Ireland, it is crucial to understand England, from whom Ireland derives much of its history and culture. England had always been the dominant force on Ireland's neighboring island, Britain, and had emerged not only as a European power but also as a regional rival and threat to Ireland, as well as Wales and Scotland. Wales was conquered by England in the 13th century AD, and Scotland and England jointly came under the rule of King James in 1603. Ireland was also subject to English incursions, starting when the Normans invaded England in 1066 and then Ireland in 1169. Catholic England took direct control over some of Ireland through a grant from the Pope, who didn't technically control the land but claimed it under the church, as most Irish people were Catholics. Still, most of Ireland came under the rule of Irish and assimilated Norman lords, who soon consolidated their power and created numerous kingdoms, such as Munster, Connacht, Leinster, and Ulster, which eventually became the four traditional provinces of Ireland. English control was greatly reduced and became limited to a small area in the East of Ireland surrounding Dublin, known as the Pale.

In the 1530s, the infamous English King Henry VIII separated England from the Catholic Church and adopted Protestantism as England's official branch of Christianity. This made him a heretic and earned him an excommunication from the Church. As a result, powers the Church held no longer extended to him, including the Lordship England had been given over Ireland. To strengthen his grip over Ireland, Henry decided to declare the island a kingdom with himself as King and launched an invasion of the island in 1542. The Brits aimed to assimilate the Irish, impose Anglican Protestantism over the Catholic island, and ban Catholicism completely. By 1603, England completed its conquest of Ireland and the Flight of Ulster's Earls in 1607 paved the way for English colonization of Ulster, the province in Ireland's North. Large swathes of Brits flocked to Ulster and established plantations, which changed the religious demographic there significantly. The province thus became majority Protestant.

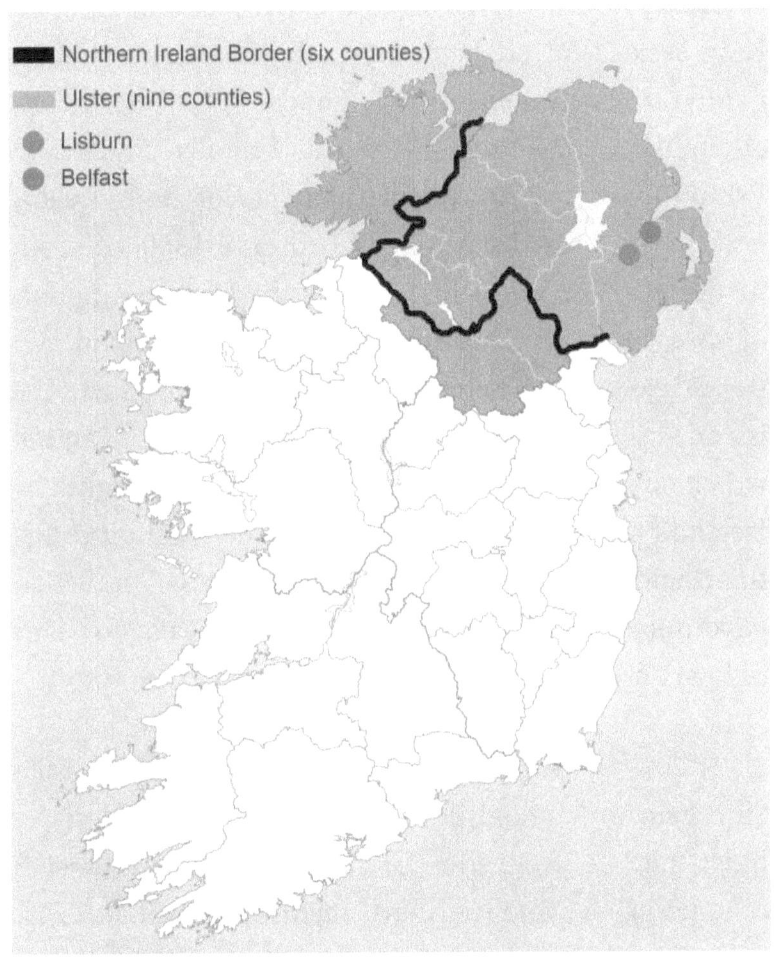

Map of Ireland with counties outlined. Ulster is shaded; Northern Ireland encompasses 6/9 Ulster counties.

"Ireland began to suffer severely under British rule; the Penal Laws passed by Britain cracked down on Catholics and banned them from all public offices. Barring brief periods of Catholic rule, such as the Irish Confederates in the 1640s and early 50s, and Catholic King James II of England, the Catholic nation remained firmly in Protestant British hands. In 1798, Ireland attempted a rebellion, which was brutally crushed by Britain. In response, the parliaments of both Ireland and Britain passed the Acts of Union in 1800, officially merging Ireland with Britain into the United Kingdom of Great Britain and Ireland. Although Ireland was treated somewhat better, it wasn't much comfort. The island suffered through tragedies like the Potato Famine, which killed 1 million people, roughly an eighth of Ireland's population, and caused another million to flee the island for places like the United States. The British government's complete inaction led to calls for land reform and, eventually Irish independence.

Following World War I, the pro-independence party Sinn Fein won a landslide election in 1918 and declared independence from the UK. Britain declared a state of emergency, and tensions rapidly intensified. Irish guerrillas like the Irish Republican Army (IRA) started attacks on British institutions and Britain's control in Leinster, Connacht, and Munster waned. This blossomed into a war to gain independence from Britain. Ireland won, and Sinn Fein politicians declared independence as the Irish Free State in 1922. However, independence came at a cost. Six of nine counties in Protestant-majority Ulster voted to stay in union with the Crown, breaking off from the island and becoming Northern Ireland. Thousands of Irish people were killed in the War for Independence and the ensuing civil war between the Irish Free State's government, who had agreed to the partition, and the IRA, who rejected it outright and wanted to reunify the island. The Irish Free State won the conflict, permanently dividing Ireland.

Since the division, Irish culture has been significantly impacted on both parts of the island. In the 1960s, a period in Irish history known as The Troubles started, in which elements sympathetic to a United Ireland started an insurgency that lasted until the 1990s. These forces included remnants of the IRA, such as the "Provisional IRA," "Official IRA," "Continuity IRA," "Real IRA," Irish National Liberation Army (INLA), and Irish People's Liberation Organisation (IPLO). More than 3,000 people were killed due to the disturbance, and combatants on all fronts—those supporting Irish unification, those supporting a continued union of Northern Ireland with Britain, and even those advocating for Northern Irish independence—were responsible for atrocities that shocked the public in Ireland, the United Kingdom, and abroad. One of the most infamous examples, and one that turned much of Ireland's Catholic population against the Brits, took place on "Bloody Sunday" in 1972, when British soldiers shot 26 unarmed civilians, killing 14, in Londonderry, Northern Ireland. Organizations such as NORAID were established in the United States and other nations with large populations of Irish descent, sending funds to rebel groups and intensifying the fighting."

Direct violence wasn't the only issue that plagued Irish people during the Troubles. Many people were impacted mentally and emotionally as a direct result of the violence they witnessed and often endured. On top of this, the whole social fabric of Northern Ireland as a whole was greatly disturbed. Communities were razed, homelessness ran rampant, and social irregularities, such as higher rates of teenage alcoholism, illegitimate pregnancies, and antisocial behaviors, were reported among people born and brought up in the backdrop of The Troubles.

Although the division happened in the early 20th century and the violence ended before the 21st, the division of Ireland continues to affect the region in many ways. For one, the partition of the island into North and South was not the only partition that occurred. "Peace Lines" or "Peace Walls" set up in Belfast (Northern Ireland's capital) during the Troubles divide predominantly Unionist and Protestant neighborhoods from predominantly

Republican and Catholic ones. Northern Ireland's government has started removing peace walls, but many residents of separated neighborhoods fear that the walls may still be necessary due to potential sporadic violence.

Billboard in Northern Ireland trying to encourage people there to vote against Brexit, which would cause Ireland to be divided between EU and non-EU areas

The United Kingdom and Ireland were historically both members of the European Union, but the UK decided to withdraw from the bloc in 2020 in a move known as Brexit, which was opposed by a majority of Northern Irish citizens. Today, many people wish for the unification of Ireland, but this is unfortunately far from happening today.

05

India – A Scarred Civilization

Let's now turn our attention to the Indian subcontinent, a region with great diversity and culture. Today, the region comprises the nations of India, Pakistan, Bangladesh, Nepal, Bhutan, Sri Lanka, and Maldives. Much like Africa, the subcontinent was once comprised of hundreds of independent nations, which were lumped together when the British Empire conquered the region and then separated upon the landmass's partition and independence. The British Empire separated the territory into the nations of India and Pakistan by religion, with India being comprised of the Hindu and Sikh-majority areas of the British Raj, and Pakistan encompassing the Muslim-majority North-West Frontier Province, Sindh, Balochistan, and half of the provinces of Punjab and Bengal. The partition and ensuing chaos resulted in mass migrations, incidents of violence, and longstanding tensions that caused conflict, war, and mistrust between India and Pakistan for decades.

In 1757, the British East India Company fought the Battle of Plassey against Bengal, a semi-autonomous province of the waning Mughal Empire and a region in the east of the Indian subcontinent. The East India Company annexed Bengal and began gaining more territory in the region. At the time, India was a patchwork of nations, ranging from large empires to small principalities. Some of the larger nations included the Mughal Empire, the Maratha Empire, and

Hyderabad State. However, most of these nations were plagued with a host of problems, including weak rulers, internal corruption, and raids from their neighbors. As a result, the British were able to wage a series of conflicts against each of these states and take near-complete control over all of them. By the 1850s, most of the Indian subcontinent remained firmly under Company rule, either directly or indirectly, through states that swore allegiance to the Crown. Some small lands were controlled by Portugal or France as well. After a large-scale, ultimately failed rebellion within the British Indian Army, the British Crown assumed direct control of the territory and governed it completely. Soon, the people of India became victims of the harsh British regime, which siphoned their resources, killed millions of people, and treated Indians as lower-class savages. Indians were conscripted into the British Army and made to fight in wars they had no part in, such as World War I. In the disastrous Gallipoli Campaign of World War I, which saw Britain, France, and Russia attempt to invade the Ottoman Empire from the Dardanelles, nearly 2,000 Indian soldiers were killed.

It quickly became clear to Indians across the subcontinent that the undesirable British Raj had to go. Leaders such as Mahatma Gandhi, Subhas Chandra Bose, and the Indian National Congress Party worked tirelessly to protest government policies and maltreatment, encourage their countrymen to join the independence movement, and in some cases, carry out violent attacks. The British hold over the subcontinent, though firm, gradually began to weaken. In World War II, the British Empire was dealt a serious blow. Fighting Germany and Japan during the war had greatly weakened the once-glorious Britain. While Germany dealt them severe blows at home, the Japanese invaded several of their colonies, such as Burma and Malaya, which greatly lessened Britain's hold in these places. In some regions, the people were given limited home rule by the Japanese. However, the most severe damage occurred just following the war, when the United States and the Soviet Union became the world's two superpowers, decrying colonial empires as unnecessary and barbaric. The UK was thus forced to withdraw from most of its colonies, including India, Burma, Palestine, and Jordan, among others.

Unfortunately, independence for India came at a cost. Although protests had been ongoing in every part of India, the movements were not all connected. As mentioned previously, some protests were civil, while others were violent. Some were regional, while others were national. Many of them followed a specific ideology, such as socialism, which was the thought process followed by Bhagat Singh, Chandra Shekhar Azad, and parties like the Hindustan Socialist

Republican Organization. Some Indians didn't care for independence at all, like the governments of some existing states that had sworn allegiance to the Crown. These princely states knew that they were too weak to survive without British administration, and so their kings wanted to remain British subjects. However, the most prominent dissidents within the independence movement were those led by Muhammad Ali Jinnah and the All-India Muslim League, who sought a separate nation for India's Muslims.

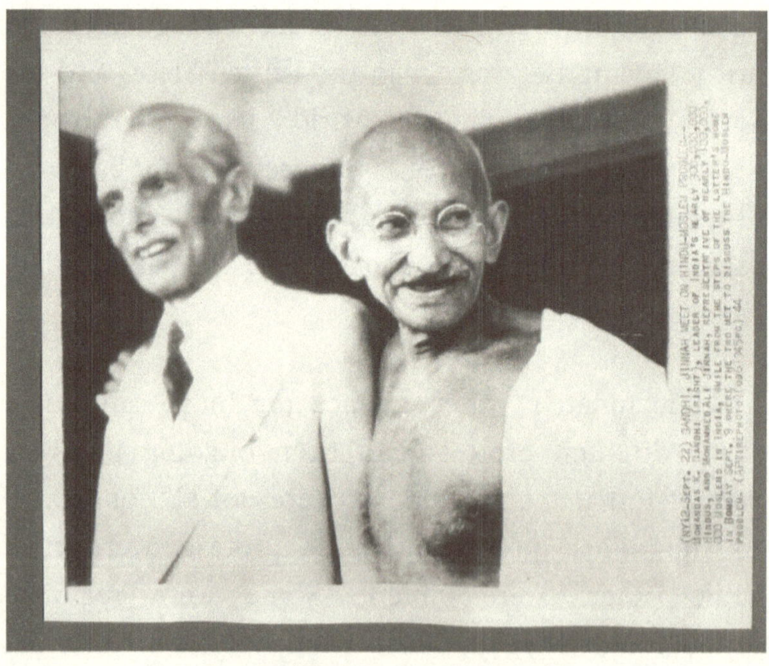

Gandhi with Jinnah in Mumbai

Islam, though originating in Arabia, had been one of India's largest religions for centuries, behind Hinduism. It first reached the subcontinent from Arab and Persian invasions, such as those of the Umayyad Caliphate led by Muhammad bin Qasim. For many centuries, in fact, the Mughals and other Turko-Muslim dynasties controlled the entire subcontinent and pursued aggressive policies of Islamization, though they were never able to convert more than a minority of people living on the subcontinent. The western parts of the subcontinent, including Sindh, Balochistan, Punjab, Kashmir, and Pashtunistan, resultantly had majority Muslim populations. There were also sizable Muslim populations in Bengal, Awadh, and other regions in India. Muhammad Ali Jinnah became the leader of a movement to establish Pakistan, a state for South Asia's Muslims. Started by Syed Ahmad Khan, Muhammad Iqbal, and other thinkers, this movement had been ongoing for quite some time but gained significant relevance in the 1930s. The movement was opposed by many organizations, including the Indian National Congress and even some Muslim organizations such as the All-India Azad Muslim Conference.

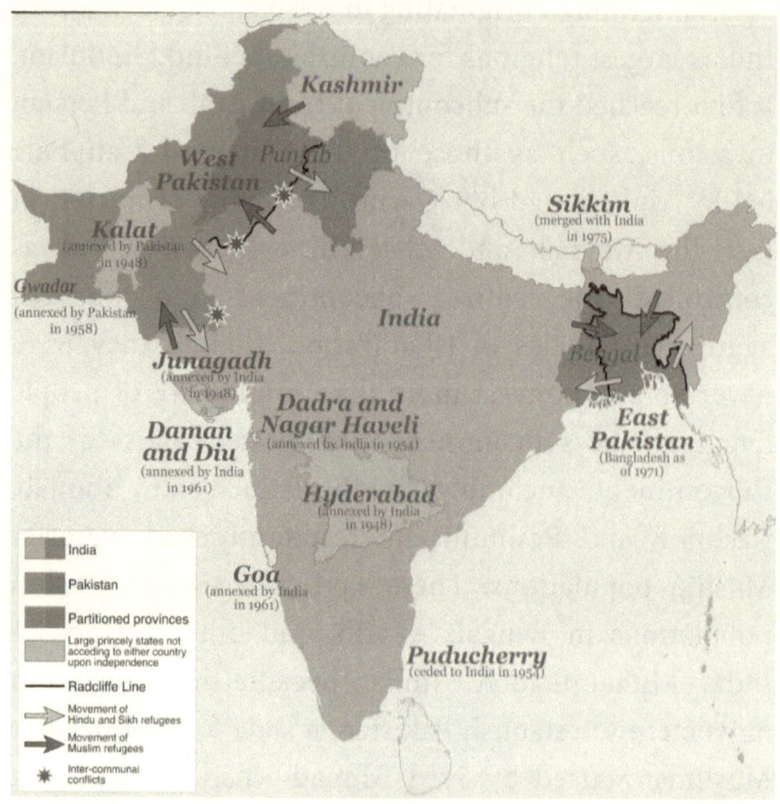

Map of colonial India at independence. Punjab and Bengal were partitioned between the two new nations. Hyderabad and Junagadh (and other territories) were annexed into India, while Kalat went to Pakistan. Kashmir remains contested.

In 1947, when the British opted to leave the subcontinent, the land was partitioned. Not only was this done due to the religious sentiments of India's Muslims, but also due to Britain's policy of "divide and rule," which allowed them to weaken nations and impose control over them for longer periods of time. A separate Pakistan was created out of the Sindhi, Baloch, Pashtun, and half of the Bengali and Punjabi parts of the subcontinent. The rest went to the new Republic of India, and the princely states were left to join whichever nation they chose. The ensuing mass migrations killed over a million people and displaced tens of millions, as Muslims in the Hindu-majority provinces flocked to Pakistan and Hindus in the Muslim-majority regions went to India. Riots, killings, and rapes were committed particularly in Bengal and Punjab, the two regions that had been divided between the two new nations.

The princely states were another issue. Most of the states were small and immediately acceded to the nation they found themselves in or near. But some of them, including Hyderabad, Junagadh, and Kashmir, were as large and populous as some independent nations. Their rulers also had religious differences with the nations they were adjacent to. Therefore, they tried to resist integration into India or Pakistan for as long as possible.

Hyderabad was located completely within India, with no access to the coast, which made integration relatively easy. Yet, it did not come without its hurdles. Hyderabad's Muslim Nizam, or ruler, was so rich and prestigious that he was on the cover of Time magazine in 1937. He presided over a powerful state that encompassed 16 million people (at the time almost 1% of the world population), and as a result, had more power than most kings in India at the time. He did not want to accede to the Hindu-majority India despite having an overwhelmingly Hindu populace. Hyderabad was too far from Pakistan to have any chance at acceding there, so the Nizam decided to remain independent. In the meantime, he removed the Indian troops stationed near the capital and continued to fight a Communist militia that had plagued the state. India, fearing the establishment of a Communist nation in its backyard, invaded and annexed Hyderabad.

Kashmir, a state located in the Northern reaches of the subcontinent, was a much bigger issue. The state bordered both India and Pakistan. The king was Hindu, but the population was majority Muslim. Initially, the king wished to remain independent, but Pakistan did not let that happen, launching an invasion into Kashmir in October 1947. The Kashmiri king quickly acceded to India, and India began repelling Pakistani forces until 1948 when a ceasefire was declared that placed almost a third of Kashmir under Pakistani control. This war took the lives of more than 5,000 people and injured nearly 15,000 more. To this day, Kashmir remains fiercely contested between India and Pakistan, and multiple wars have been fought over the territory.

Almost immediately, the effects of the partition began to rear their ugly heads. India was officially a secular nation whose constitution guaranteed the rights of all people to practice any religion. Pakistan was an Islamic republic that also nominally guaranteed the same rights, but attacks against Hindu, Sikh, and Christian people happened almost every day. This low tolerance for minorities in Pakistan quickly became a problem between the two countries. India and Pakistan have fought four wars since independence, including three over Kashmir. The remaining war, which occurred in 1971, is another perfect example of the ill effects that the partition had on the subcontinent as a whole.

Pakistan was made up of multiple regions or parts of regions: Punjab, Sindh, Balochistan, Pashtunistan (or Khyber Pakhtunkhwa), Kashmir, and Bengal. All of these regions are found in the Western part of South Asia, and they are all contiguous. Well, except for Bengal. Bengal, located in the Eastern part of the Indian subcontinent, was split between India and Pakistan due to its large numbers of both Hindus and Muslims. Although it was culturally distinct from the Western Muslim-majority provinces, it was split and parts given to Pakistan due to the religious demographic there. Named East Bengal, Pakistani Bengal was renamed "East Pakistan" in 1955 to metaphorically link it with the rest of the country. However, systematic issues were prevalent in East Pakistan. The most significant issue, and the one that arguably caused most of the problems that will be mentioned shortly, was a general belief among the West Pakistani elite that they were racially superior to East Pakistanis. Jinnah declared Urdu to be the only official language of Pakistan, while Bengal was far and away the most Bengali-speaking and least Urdu-speaking province in Pakistan. On top of this, most of Pakistan's government funds were allocated to the West, leaving the East undeveloped, hungry, and economically disadvantaged. Bengalis were also underrepresented in Pakistan's military and government.

Bengali Muslims often identified with the Pakistan movement before the partition of India. As a matter of fact, Bangladesh's national hero and first president, Sheikh Mujibur Rahman, would supposedly ride on his bike to listen to Muhammad Ali Jinnah speak. But Bengalis soon realized they valued their ethnic background a lot more than their religion. In 1970, Bengal's Awami League enjoyed a landslide victory in the national elections, winning 167 out of 169 seats. Rahman, their leader, urged people to protest the Pakistani regime and to fight. Pakistan's gross neglect following the 1970 Bhola Cyclone in Bengal, in which 300,000 people were killed, as well as the dreadful Bangladesh genocide in 1971, which resulted in up to 3,000,000 deaths and 400,000 rapes, encouraged East Pakistan to start a full-scale civil war, which India eventually joined on the Bengalis' side. Pakistan was defeated, and East Pakistan declared independence as *Bangladesh*.

The partition of India continues to be a catalyst for extreme tension in South Asia. Although the days in which India and Pakistan fought four wars are long gone, relations are still hostile. Kashmir continues to be warred over, and both sides have accused each other of providing aid to separatist elements in either nation (India to Baloch, Sindhi, Pashtun rebels, etc., and Pakistan to Sikh/Muslim separatists). In India, it is very hard for Pakistanis to get visas to visit, much less go and actually stay there. The entire border between both countries remains tightly fenced and closely guarded by border patrols. Kashmir remains a point of contention, and with recent Indian actions to revoke Kashmir's constitutional autonomy, the state has been brought closer to India, angering Pakistan. Pakistan's continued support for terror outfits, both in India and abroad, is a major sore spot. And it's not just tensions that were caused by the division. Rather, the culture in both places completely changed as a result.

In India, language, writing, food, and religion are all incredibly different from Pakistan. Although Urdu and Hindi are similar, and Punjabi is more or less the same language irrespective of the boundary, the separation has led to the growth and development of various unique dialects and variations of each language. India and Pakistan have somewhat veered in two different directions, culturally, politically, and economically.

Starting culturally, Pakistan utilizes a Perso-Arabic script to write its languages, including Punjabi, Urdu, Pashto, and others. India uses mostly scripts that have been in place for longer, like Devanagari to write Hindi, Marathi, Gujarati, etc. The nation is obviously Muslim compared to Hindu-majority India, and, as such, observes different holidays and traditions than most Indians.

Politically, it's a similar story. Upon independence, India was governed by Prime Minister Jawaharlal Nehru, a close friend and associate of Gandhi's. The Indian National Congress became the main political party of post-independence India, and Nehru became its leader after Gandhi's assassination in 1948. Following Nehru's death in 1962, Congress leadership was taken over by his daughter Indira Gandhi (no relation to Mahatma Gandhi), who became Prime Minister in 1966. Allegations of cronyism, nepotism, and corruption weakened Congress' image in the latter 20th century and paved the way for parties like the Bharatiya Jana Sangh, which eventually morphed into the Bharatiya Janata Party (BJP), to gain widespread support. Despite the obvious issues that plagued the Indian government since 1947, such as nepotism, scandals like the Bofors scandal in the 1980s and 90s, and occasional abuse of powers like Indira Gandhi's Emergency in which constitutional rights were suspended, the nation has always remained a free, secular, and fair democracy. Pakistan, on the other hand, has seen multiple military dictatorships, presidents overthrown or executed, and coup d'états that have prevented peaceful transfers of power. In fact, Pakistan's first peaceful civilian transfer of power was in 2013, 66 years after gaining independence. The nation has had three iterations of their constitution, as earlier versions would be suspended by dictators. Leaders and former leaders like Zulfikar Ali Bhutto, Muhammad Zia-ul-Haq, and Benazir Bhutto were executed or died under mysterious circumstances, while the nation recently saw Prime Minister Imran Khan controversially removed and charged with various crimes against the state.

The GDP difference between the two nations is still very high. India's GDP as of 2022 is $3.469 trillion, while its PPP is $8,293. Pakistan's GDP is $376.5 billion, and its PPP is $6,662. This means that India's cumulative GDP is 9 times higher, while the population is only about 6 times higher. This allows India to spend far more on welfare programs, the military, and investments. Per year, India spends the equivalent of $76.6 billion on their military, while Pakistan spends a yearly $11.3 billion. Currently, Indian rupees (the currency) are worth much more than Pakistani rupees, with one US Dollar being equal to 83 INR , or 278 PKR.

Some believe that a reunification would fix many of the problems outlined above. Many do advocate for the reunification of the Indian subcontinent. Unfortunately, this is a dream that is far farther away from fruition than it appears at this time. India and Pakistan are two nations that developed completely different cultures after the partition, and as a result, unification would involve the reversal of years of cultural shifts, hostilities, and tensions between the two states.

06

Koreas – The Division of a People

Unlike previous partitions, the partition of Korea didn't happen as a result of ethnic or social conflict but rather politics. The division of Korea remains one of the most impactful divisions in modern history, separating a nation into two distinct countries, North Korea and South Korea, where, despite ethnic similarities, the government, culture, and economy couldn't be more different.

For centuries, Korea had been an independent nation under the rule of multiple indigenous dynasties, such as the Goryeo, Silla, and Joseon. They had managed to retain independence for most of their history due to a strong army and by being tributaries of powerful empires like China. However, in 1910, the Korean Empire (encompassing North and South Korea) was conquered and colonized by the Empire of Japan. The Japanese overthrew the monarchy and governed the country directly. The Imperialist Japanese used Korea, which had a land border with China, as a military base to station troops and launch attacks into China. In 1937, one such attack became a full-fledged war, as Japan marched into China, which was already weak due to an ongoing civil war. The Pacific Theater of World War II was underway, and it truly kicked off with Japan's bombing of Pearl Harbor. The US, UK, and USSR fought to defeat Japan and strip it of its colonial possessions, including Korea.

When Japan's imperialist ambitions were quelled, the Korean Peninsula was divided between the Americans and the Soviets, with the US occupying the South and the Soviet Union taking over the North. Although the plan was to stabilize the peninsula, eventually reunite it, and hold free and fair elections for the government, this plan never came to fruition. The Soviets set up a Communist regime in the North, headed by Kim Il-Sung, while the US established an anti-Communist government under Syngman Rhee. The Cold War between the US and USSR was beginning, and Korea was one major flashpoint of conflict between the two superpowers, starting when the North invaded the South with Soviet aid. Seoul, the South's capital, was captured in a matter of days, and it looked like the North would win. However, the United Nations deployed a task force, comprised mostly of American troops, to fight on South Korea's behalf.

South Korean troops preparing to fight the invading Chinese Communist forces

The tide of the war began to turn in the anti-Communist South's favor, as the communists were pushed almost to the Chinese border. But just when it looked like the anti-communists would prevail, the Communist Chinese government that formed in the wake of China's civil war feared that its own national security could be put in jeopardy if the UN Task Force continued. As a result, China sent nearly 1.5 million troops into Korea to fight for the North. After some more back-and-forth, the war reached a stalemate and a ceasefire was declared, roughly at the same border the two Koreas had prior to the war.

Although the fighting stopped, the tension between the two sides continued for decades. The US and its allies continued to support the South, and the Soviets and their allies the North. The war technically hasn't ended even today, as North and South Korea have emerged as two completely different nations. The South, after a period of dictatorships, became a capitalist democracy and is today one of the "Four Asian Tigers," four East Asian nations with some of the most successful and quickly-growing economies in the region. North Korea has been ruled by the Kim dynasty since its foundation, Kim Il-sung's descendants. The North is run as an open-air prison, and North Korean citizens are completely cut off from the outside world. Quality of life in the North is extremely poor, the government carefully controls every facet of North Korean people's lives, and any opposition or attempt to escape is met with execution of the perpetrators and their families. The nation has ownership of nuclear weapons, which is illegal under the Nuclear Non-Proliferation Treaty (which North Korea withdrew from). Although the North formally abandoned communism in 2009, it still functions very similarly to a Communist nation, with no private ownership and complete state control of all assets.

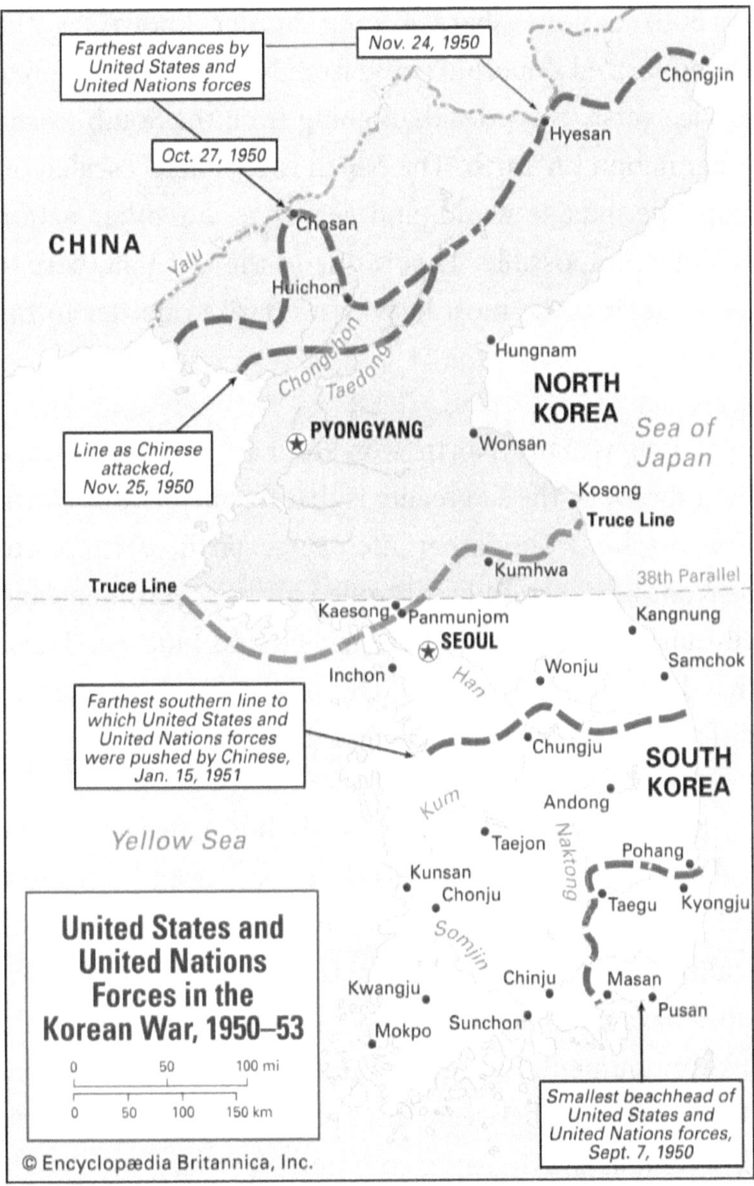

Map of Korea from division to now. At first divided along the 38th parallel, Korea was later split along a truce line that gained South Korea territory but gave up the historical city of Kaesong to the North.

Both nations share a long border known as the Demilitarized Zone, but going from North to South Korea, or vice versa, is harder than going from the South to any other nation on Earth. The North is completely sealed off from the outside world, and escape to any other nation is almost impossible. This is due to the fact that, despite its name, it is the most heavily militarized border in the world.

Though many North Koreans have tried to escape their dystopia, the sad reality is that the majority of North Koreans know no other life. Since birth, each North Korean's life is carefully controlled by the government, and all outside information is restricted and blocked. Those that do manage to escape often find it difficult to adjust to different ways of life outside North Korea.

Korean unification is a very hotly debated topic today that has varying levels of support from both sides. While both sides would like a unification of Korea, the reality is that it is far easier said than done. The two sides have complete fundamental differences that would take monumental efforts to resolve. Firstly, the system of government between the two nations is completely different, as previously mentioned. Secondly, the people have become fundamentally different in culture and way of life, including what information they are given and even their language to an extent. Thirdly, the two nations are different in general. What that means is that the infrastructure in both nations is meant for two different things. While South Korea is built as a free, capitalist nation with connections to the rest of the world, North Korea is an isolated dictatorship whose resources are used to build up the country's military. This can even be seen in their roads. Many North Koreans are too poor to buy a car, and the roads there are built very wide and large to allow tanks and other military machinery to pass through. Support for unification in the South is dwindling, too. While historically the number of South Koreans that wanted unification was high, most do not want reunification today, as there would be severe economic consequences. For one, the influx of North Koreans to South Korea would cause more pressure in the South's already competitive housing and job markets. Additionally, South Koreans would likely be obliged to pay higher taxes for many years to bring the North at least somewhat up to the South's standards, as there is a complete difference in infrastructure and development between the two Koreas. In fact, if you look at Korea at night on Google Maps, you can see South Korea, China, and Japan completely lit up, while North Korea is almost completely dark.

The most important issue, though, is that neither country can agree on a course of action to unify the peninsula. It would have to be governed under one government, and neither side wants a government under the other. This has severe implications not only for the two Koreas but also for the world's major powers. For the US, an entirely Kim-controlled or similarly-run Korea would be an antagonistic dictatorship that would threaten world peace at a grander scale than it currently does. For Russia or China, a US-aligned Korea on their borders would be disastrous, and Russia would not want to lose North Korea like it did East Germany or the rest of the Eastern bloc. Besides even the most basic argument of international balance of power and security, trade between the world and Korea would change drastically depending on which government ran the reunified peninsula. If a democratic, capitalist government like the South's was to take power, the South would immediately gain access to the North's vast natural resources, like the millions of tons of uranium ore within North Korea. In fact, Goldman Sachs back in 2009 estimated that a United Korean economy could surpass the economies of both Germany and Japan to be one of the largest in the world. Western democratic nations like the US would almost certainly be the main beneficiaries of a unified Korea under the South. If the North was to rule the peninsula, though, it would impose its harsh laws on all Koreans, and would most probably use the South's vast resources to further their own nuclear weapons program. Trade to and from Korea would be almost completely cut off for any nation viewed unfavorably by the Kim regime, which would be disastrous for the global economy.

Today, the two nations are completely hostile to one another, as North Korea views South Korea as a West-aligned traitor, while the South sees the North as an evil dictatorship. Neither nation recognizes the other, and both claim the entire Korean Peninsula and its inhabitants on both sides as their citizens.

Still, the two nations historically worked together to try to unify the peninsula. They had occasional cross-border diplomacy and had even sent Unified Korean teams to the Olympics. However, in the past few months, the North has completely pivoted on this approach and gone back to considering the South an outright enemy they want nothing to do with. As such, they have carried out missile tests near the South to try and scare them, they blew up a building South Korea created in their territory for reunification, and they've destroyed unification monuments across North Korea, showing their hostility to a peaceful and prosperous unification.

Clearly, Korea's division changed the entire world. Today, the Korean people remain divided, with the ⅓ of them living in the North being denied basic human rights on a daily basis. The land remains a fiercely contested Cold War-era battleground between the US and her adversaries, particularly China and Russia. North Korea, though isolated from most of the world, still makes its presence felt by its repeated threats to nations like South Korea and the United States. South Korea has become one of the most developed nations in the world, being known for innovations in medicine, biotechnology, and automobiles, among other things. Hopefully, the two Koreas can one day unify peacefully and safely. However, this is difficult and will take a great deal of dialogue and commitment from not just both Koreas but the entire international community as a whole.

07

USSR – The Collapse of a Superpower

Arguably, the most impactful partition in modern history is the partition of the Soviet Union. The former superpower comprised the nations of Russia, Ukraine, Belarus, Moldova, Latvia, Estonia, Lithuania, Azerbaijan, Armenia, Georgia, Kazakhstan, Kyrgyzstan, Uzbekistan, Tajikistan, and Turkmenistan, making it by far the largest nation on the planet. Founded in 1922, the Soviet Union was the Communist successor to the great Russian Empire, one of the most powerful nations in Europe and the world for many years. What differentiated Russia from other imperial powers, however, was its contiguity. While empires like those of the British or French spanned multiple pieces of territory on multiple continents, Russia stretched uninterrupted from Warsaw in the West to Alaska in the East. It also encompassed the Caucasus and Central Asia, which gave it a very racially diverse population. But how did Russia, once a collection of duchies and principalities in Eastern Europe, become as large and unique as it did?

Modern Russia has its origins in the Kievan Rus', a medieval polity founded in AD 840. Ruled by the Rurikid dynasty, its namesake first ruler, Rurik, was a member of the Varangians, a group of people descended from Vikings that settled in Eastern Europe. The Rus', based in Kiev (now Kyiv, Ukraine), was a powerful polity that eventually succumbed to a Mongol Invasion and fractured into various small states. However, the states, led by the Grand Duchy of Moscow, were able to remove the Mongols from the region in the 1380 Battle of Kulikovo. The states were soon consolidated under Moscow, and Grand Prince Ivan IV the Terrible was proclaimed Tsar (Russian for *Caesar*) of all Russia, establishing the Russian Tsardom. He began a process of mass expansion to Russia's west and east. While these campaigns were initially successful, Russia's brutal loss in the Livonian War resulted in the loss of territories in Estonia, Livonia, Ingria, and Russia proper. Living standards across the Tsardom declined, and Ivan became more and more despotic. He established the first Russian standing army, purged his government, and even murdered his oldest son and heir, Ivan Ivanovich. He perpetrated the Novgorod massacre, and Moscow was burned by Tatars supported by the Ottomans. Importantly, Ivan also began the conquest of Siberia.

Ivan was himself a Rurikid, but his dynasty lasted only until 1598 before being replaced by the Romanov dynasty, a family with German roots. For the next few hundred years, Russia expanded more and more, extending beyond the Ural Mountains into Siberia. The Turkic Khanates on Russia's frontier, remnants of the Mongol Empire, were annexed into Russia, including Sibir, Astrakhan, and Kazan. As Russia grew, it extended beyond the Ural Mountains, which form part of the geographical border between the continents of Europe and Asia. Russia soon gained power and, in 1721, reconquered its former lands in Northern and Eastern Europe. It expanded into the Caucasus region, acquiring several territories through wars with Turkey, Persia, and several small states in the region. These lands included Chechnya, Dagestan, Circassia, and Ossetia, as well as the modern-day independent nations of Armenia, Azerbaijan, and Georgia. Russia also advanced into Central Asia, annexing several lands that make up the modern-day countries of Kazakhstan, Kyrgyzstan, Uzbekistan, Tajikistan, and Turkmenistan.

It's clear that these regions greatly increased Russia's ethnic composition; the empire was now home to Russians, Ukrainians, Belarusians, Poles, Romanians, Estonians, Latvians, Lithuanians, Finns, Swedes, Germans, and Rusyns in the European portion alone. In Asia, the Empire contained Russians, Armenians, Georgians, Azerbaijanis, Kazakhs, Kyrgyz, Uzbeks, Tajiks, Turkmens, Tatars, Bashkirs, Tuvans, Chechens, Koreans, and hundreds more races and ethnic groups. Russia was one of the largest and most powerful nations and by far the largest contiguous empire in the world.

Map of the Soviet Union with each ethnicity-based SSR shown. Each SSR would go on to become its own nation, with Russia being the largest and most powerful.

However, as is the case with most large nations, internal problems very quickly became external problems. Persecution of minorities, particularly Muslims and Jews, by the government was rampant. Jews, for example, were the target of various pogroms and were only permitted to live in a small portion of the empire, known as the *Jewish Pale.* Poverty was widespread, and the Russian nobility and monarchy seemingly led lavish lifestyles, even as their nation lagged behind the rest of Europe politically, militarily, and economically. Resentment began to build among some, though the *Okhrana*, the Tsar's secret police force, repressed any opposition.

This discontent became very apparent even with ordinary Russians, and soon, the entire nation, which was already going through World War I, found itself in the midst of a full-scale civil war. The royal government and successive republic were overthrown and replaced with a Communist government headed by Vladimir Lenin. Within a few years, the nation was organized into the USSR or the Union of Soviet Socialist Republics.

Following World War II, the Soviet Union was organized into fifteen Soviet Socialist Republics based on ethnic composition, the largest being the Russian SFSR. Not unlike previous examples of partitions, this one was done very haphazardly. The republics' borders followed few historical borders and instead were created for political purposes, mainly so the central Soviet government could have some degree of control over their regions. One example is Moldova, formerly known as Bessarabia, which was populated by ethnic Romanians. The southern part of Bessarabia, which adjoined the Black Sea, was cut off and integrated into Ukraine, while the rest, now known as Moldova, was given a tiny strip of land east of the Dniester River known as Transnistria, which was formerly a part of the Ukrainian SSR and had a Russian/Ukrainian majority. Russians were encouraged to settle in other republics, such as Ukraine and Kazakhstan. In Central Asia, particularly in Kyrgyzstan, Uzbekistan, and Tajikistan, borders were created based on ethnic composition. However, these borders were extremely detailed. Villages that were next to each other but contained different peoples were assigned to different Republics, creating innumerable territorial disputes. If one looks at a map of Central Asia today, one can see the absolute border gore that was created as a result of Soviet policy. For instance, the Fergana Valley, a historical region containing many important historical sites and cities such as Kokand, Osh, and Khujand, was partitioned rather oddly between the Kyrgyz, Uzbek, and Tajik SSRs.

Discontented with living under this Communist dictatorship, each republic withdrew from the USSR one by one, resulting in its total collapse in 1991. However, there were many conflicts that resulted from the collapse. The Soviet Union had a policy in which they would create autonomous regions within their fifteen constituent republics, such as the Nagorno-Karabakh autonomous oblast in Azerbaijan, which was home to mostly ethnic Armenians, or the Chechno-Ingush autonomous republic in Caucasian Russia, home to Chechens and Ingush, two Turkic, mostly Muslim peoples. When the Soviet Union collapsed, these people immediately became minorities in the countries they found themselves in. Nagorno-Karabakh quickly became contested between Azerbaijan, which had political ownership over the territory, and Armenia, whose people lived there and wanted to join Armenia. A bitter conflict took place between the two nations and was resolved only last year when Azerbaijan finally took control of the region and all Armenian residents fled. This one conflict claimed the lives of almost 50,000 people.

In Chechnya and Ingushetia, a state called the Chechen Republic of Ichkeria was set up and proclaimed independence from Russia in 1991. Though Ingushetia eventually broke off and rejoined Russia, Chechnya continued to enjoy de facto independence until 1994, when Russian troops entered the republic, captured the capital Grozny, and started the First Chechen War. Although Russia had a significant military advantage, the Chechens were able to recapture Grozny in 1996 and once again retain independence until 1999, when Russia kicked off the Second Chechen War, fully recapturing and reintegrating Chechnya with the help of pro-Russian Chechens. This conflict claimed the lives of anywhere between 100,000-200,000 people and left hundreds of thousands more injured or displaced, many of them civilians who were targeted in some attacks by both sides.

Another such conflict was the Crimean conflict between Ukraine and Russia. In 1954, the Soviet Union had just won World War II less than a decade ago. During the war, Crimea's ethnic Tatar population was accused by the Soviet central government of collaborating with the Nazi Germans and were therefore deported from Crimea. The peninsula was repopulated with Russians and Ukrainians and was a part of Russia. However, in 1954, it was transferred to Ukraine on the occasion of the 300th anniversary of Ukraine's union with Russia. After the collapse of the Soviet Union, Russia demanded that Crimea be handed over to them, declaring the 1954 transfer null and void. In a similar fashion, the Donbas region in Eastern Ukraine is home to mostly ethnic Russians. Russia, though technically absolved of any claim to Donbas since 1991, always had contentious relations with Ukraine over the territory. When pro-Russian president Viktor Yanukovych took office and instituted political and economic policies that shifted Ukraine away from the European Union and toward Russia, many Ukrainians were unhappy. As a result, the Euromaidan protests took place and resulted in Yanukovych's ouster in 2014. Following this development, Russia invaded and annexed Crimea and started pro-Russian insurgencies in two provinces in the Donbas, Donetsk and Luhansk. The longstanding tensions between Russia and Ukraine culminated in the full invasion of Ukraine in 2022, costing millions of lives.

Final Soviet Leader Mikhail Gorbachev

The partition of the former Soviet Union had a tremendous impact on the entire world. It created fifteen new nations and an onslaught of modern conflicts. Russia, the political successor to the USSR, still harbors great mistrust of the West. The West's attempts to expand NATO to the former Soviet states around Russia have drawn criticism from Moscow, who views NATO's expansion as neo-imperialism and as a threat against Russia. Russia's 2022 invasion of Ukraine was taken with the goal of preventing Ukraine's admission into NATO, which would put the bloc right at Russia's doorstep. The conflicts created as a result of this partition include the aforementioned Russo-Ukrainian War, the Nagorno-Karabakh Conflict, the Chechen War, and countless other wars and conflicts across the globe. Today, people are dying every day in Ukraine due to Russia's war there, and all of this can be traced back to the partition of the Soviet Union, along with dozens of other conflicts whose undercurrents can still be felt today.

08

Yugoslavia – A Dream That Ended in Despair

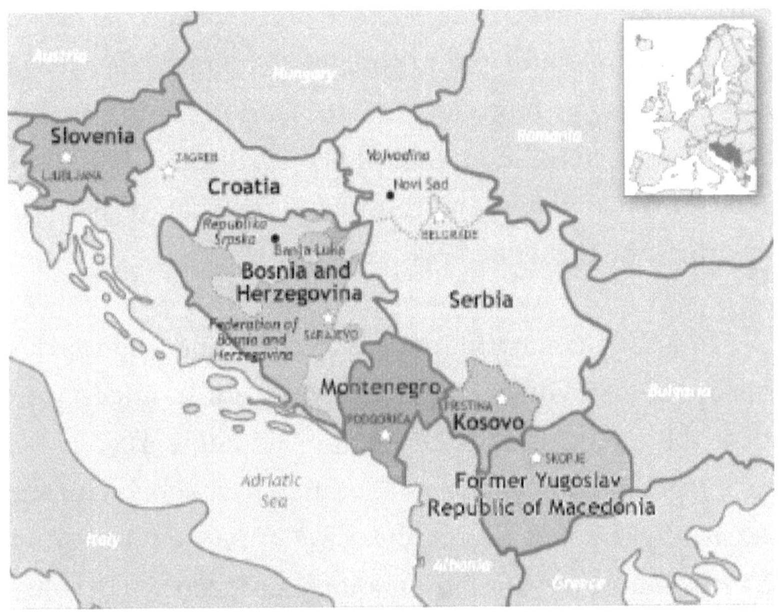

Map of each nation that once comprised Yugoslavia

By the late 80s and early '90s, the era of communism was coming to a close. The regimes of Poland, Romania, Mongolia, and several other nations around the world that were previously Communist abandoned Marxism and (in most cases) became free nations with capitalist regimes. During this time, many nations, such as the Soviet Union itself, came to an abrupt end as communism, which had suppressed any nationalist sentiment, was abandoned, and the people in the multiethnic nations were allowed the right to self-determination. Nations like the USSR, Czechoslovakia, and Yugoslavia were broken up by nationality. While the post-Soviet conflicts immediately in the wake of the USSR's collapse only extended to certain parts of the former empire, and Czechoslovakia had a completely peaceful and negotiated demerger, Yugoslavia was completely embroiled in a decade-long civil war that killed hundreds of thousands of people, displaced millions of innocent civilians, and resulted in the trials of 161 war criminals by the United Nations.

To understand the circumstances behind Yugoslavia's collapse and civil war, it is first important to understand how the nation came into being. The name *Yugoslavia*, or *Jugoslavija* in Serbo-Croatian, roughly means *Land of the South Slavs*. The Slavs are an ethnic group consisting of several groups of Europeans. They are typically divided into East Slavs (consisting of Russians, Ukrainians, Belarusians, and other groups), West Slavs (comprising Poles, Czechs, Slovaks, and other groups), and South Slavs. The South Slavs are native to the Balkan Peninsula in Southeastern Europe and contain a diverse array of ethnicities, including Serbs, Croats, Bosniaks, Montenegrins, Slovenes, Macedonians, and Bulgarians, among others.

While initially independent under kingdoms like Serbia or Bosnia, the South Slavs eventually came under the rule of one empire or another, such as the Byzantines, Ottomans, or Austro-Hungarians. Their precarious position in the Balkan Peninsula, between the Hungarians to the North, Turks and Russians to the East, Italians to the West, and Germans to the Northwest, meant that they were a battleground for various conflicts that erupted between these competing empires through the centuries. As a result of these conflicts, the subsequent drawing and redrawing of boundaries, and imposition of foreign ways of life upon them, South Slavs became fragmented and diverse. One example is in their religions. As a result of Greek Byzantine rule, peoples like the Serbs and Bulgarians adopted the Eastern Orthodox sect of Christianity. Groups like the Slovenes and Croats adopted Catholicism due to Hungarian/Austrian rule and their proximity to Italy. Meanwhile, groups like the Bosniaks and Albanians (the latter of whom aren't Slavs but are Balkan nonetheless) by and large converted to Islam as a result of Ottoman Turkish rule.

By the late 19th century, these people had become extremely discontent with their continued rule by foreigners, which had lasted several centuries by this point. Austria-Hungary and Ottoman Turkey, the two main occupying powers in the Balkans, had now become much weaker, especially the Ottomans. Many of the South Slavic people began to dream of a unified Southern Slav nation that would encompass all South Slavs and give the long-oppressed people the chance to finally govern themselves. As the Ottoman Empire crumbled from within, Bulgaria and Serbia were able to break away under new monarchies and rule themselves. Montenegro, though small and already *de facto* independent for some time, was now less at risk from the Ottomans and Austrians, and so they proclaimed themselves a Principality and later a Kingdom, which would have previously angered the great powers surrounding it. The dream of a unified South Slavic nation was now underway. Following the complete defeat of Austria-Hungary in World War I, the remaining South Slavic territories were released, and the State of Serbs, Croats, and Slovenes was established. This nation, comprising Slovenia, Croatia, and Bosnia, unified with Serbia and Montenegro to form the Kingdom of Yugoslavia. Bulgaria chose not to join the Union. The former colonial subdivisions that existed were disestablished and first replaced with *oblasts*, and then with nine *banovinas* in 1929. These *banovinas* were established in a manner that ethnicities within the Kingdom were not divided, although a *banovina* of Croatia was later carved out at the behest of Croatian politicians.

During World War II, the Axis powers Germany, Italy, Hungary, and Bulgaria invaded and split Yugoslavia. Drava, the banovina that encompassed most of modern-day Slovenia, was split between the Germans, Hungarians, and Italians. Italy annexed parts of coastal Croatia and Montenegro in accordance with Italian irredentism, and the rest of Montenegro was made a protectorate, as were parts of modern Macedonia and Serbia that had sizable Albanian populations. Bulgaria annexed the rest of Macedonia and parts of Serbia, while Hungary annexed some of Vojvodina, a historical region in Northern Serbia that had historically been part of Hungary. This left Bosnia and the core territories of Serbia and Croatia. Serbia was occupied by Germany, while Croatia and Bosnia were placed under the rule of a puppet state headed by the Croatian ultra-fascist Ustase, who committed countless war crimes against the Serb populations of Bosnia and Croatia, as well as the regions' Jewish population.

While the nation suffered under Axis occupation, guerrilla insurgents worked to bring about Yugoslav independence. The two main anti-Axis groups were the Chetniks and the Communist Partisans. The Chetniks were remnants of the old royal regime, who were initially the dominant group and were favored by the Allies. However, there were inherent issues present. Firstly, the Chetniks were pro-Serb and would commit atrocities against Croats and Muslim Bosniaks. Secondly, they were seen as elitists by many Yugoslavians, in contrast to the Partisans, whose acceptance of the poor appealed to many. Thirdly, they would occasionally collaborate with the Axis to pursue their own agendas. Lastly, and most importantly, they were simply not as effective as the Partisans. The Partisans were clearly superior in guerrilla tactics, recruiting, and diplomacy, which resulted in the Allies withdrawing support for the Chetniks and instead supporting the Partisans, headed by Marshal Josip Broz Tito.

By 1945, the Axis powers had been driven out of Yugoslavia. However, the nation emerged from the war drastically different from how it entered it. The monarchy was driven out, and a Communist regime, headed by Tito, took power. Yugoslavia was one of eight nations that became Communist following the war, with Poland, Czechoslovakia, Romania, Bulgaria, Albania, East Germany, and Hungary. Besides Yugoslavia (and to an extent Romania and Albania), these nations were almost entirely controlled by the Soviet regime. What made Yugoslavia different from the other Eastern European nations was that it was able to liberate itself independently of Soviet aid. As a result, Tito was the undisputed ruler of Yugoslavia and wasn't a figurehead put into place by Joseph Stalin. Although he pursued political relations with the Soviet-dominated Communist world as the Cold War began, the Yugoslavs and Soviets quickly became hostile. While the USSR attempted to exert its influence and demands on the Communist world, it found that it was unable to prevent Yugoslavia from pursuing directives that did not align with Soviet policy in the way it could pressure Poland or Bulgaria, for example. Notably, Tito wanted to integrate Albania into Yugoslavia, which Albania and the Soviet Union were both very worried about. Tito also supported Communist rebels in Greece that the Soviets were secretly opposed to. Stalin and Tito developed a personal animosity that consisted of repeated threats and criticisms issued to each other. Reportedly, Stalin sent multiple assassins to Yugoslavia to kill Tito.

"If you don't stop sending killers, I'll send one to Moscow, and I won't have to send another." – Tito (left) to Stalin (right)

Relations all but ended, and Yugoslavia soon found itself alone in a continent dominated by a capitalist West and Communist East. Yugoslavia had regained lands it lost during the Second World War, as well as some new territory from Italy. Tito reorganized Yugoslavia's territory into divisions based on ethnicity. These were more similar to those used before the creation of Yugoslavia. Slovenia, Bosnia-Herzegovina, and Croatia gained the same borders they had under the Austro-Hungarians. Montenegro was recreated similarly. This left the former Serbia. Its southern Macedonian-speaking part was broken off into a separate Macedonia, while the rest was kept as Serbia. However, these borders weren't perfect. There were sizable Serbian minorities in Croatia, Montenegro, and especially Bosnia-Herzegovina, and Serbia itself contained an autonomous province known as Kosovo that housed a primarily Albanian population, and the Serb-majority Vojvodina was made another Serbian autonomous province. By this point, it was clear that the dream of a unified South Slavic state was not all sunshine and rainbows as originally promised, but ethnic tensions were quelled by Tito's Communist regime, whose total power and control over Yugoslavia kept the nation together.

This changed in 1980 with Tito's death. The central government's control over each of the constituent republics diminished significantly, and soon protests for greater autonomy emerged in various parts of the nation. Serbs, who were politically the most dominant and whose republic housed the capital Belgrade, were in favor of centralization. However, the nation's other groups weren't. In the early 1980s, protests by Kosovar Albanians took place demanding greater autonomy within Serbia. This was followed by calls from Croatia and Slovenia for increased decentralization. In 1987, Slobodan Milosevic took power in Serbia and won support in Montenegro and the Serbian autonomous province of Vojvodina due to his support for Serbian dominance. Croatia and Slovenia declared independence after pro-independence parties won in Yugoslavia's first multiparty elections in 1990. This kicked off the Yugoslav Wars, which saw Serbia and Serb-aligned groups in Croatia and Bosnia fight to maintain Yugoslavia. In Bosnia-Herzegovina, Serbs made up 37% of the population and had different cultural practices and religious beliefs than their Bosniak neighbors. While Bosniaks are Muslims, speak Bosnian, and write in the Latin alphabet, Serbs are Orthodox Christians, speak Serbian, and write in the Cyrillic alphabet, which is also used by Russians and Bulgarians, among others. These differences between Serbs, Bosniaks, and Croats resulted in the Bosnian War and Croatian War, two wars that resulted in the deaths of hundreds of thousands of people and the displacement of millions more.

Another important conflict that erupted was the Kosovo War, which saw Albanian-majority Kosovo try to secede from Serbia. This resulted in the deaths of thousands and the displacement of almost a million Kosovar Albanians from Kosovo, which was widely regarded as an ethnic cleansing. In response, NATO bombed Yugoslavia, which was controversial as it was done without the approval of the United Nations.

In sum, countless extrajudicial killings, lootings, and rapes occurred, among other crimes, which prompted the United Nations to set up the International Criminal Tribunal for the former Yugoslavia, a body made to bring war criminals to justice. 161 people were indicted, including Serbian president Slobodan Milosevic himself, making this the largest criminal tribunal since World War II and associated courts. Milosevic would die in 2006, after which Montenegro peacefully seceded from Serbia. However, this wasn't the end of tensions. In 2008, Kosovo once again unilaterally declared independence from Serbia, which was internationally recognized by 104 nations. To this day, although the Balkans are mostly peaceful, there are still underlying tensions. For one, Serbia still claims Kosovo as part of its territory. Although the region has been pacified, it took millions of lives, and the dream of a unified South Slavic nation is now dead.

Epilogue

It is evident that partitions have greatly impacted the world. We've seen so many lands, nations, and peoples divided, and their cultures, ways of life, and destinies diverging completely. It is impossible and rather silly to speculate on future partitions, but what can be speculated on is the continued impact of partitions that have already occurred.

Clearly, the effects of partitions are very visible today. As mentioned previously, wars across the world continue to kill millions, many of which are by-products of division. The Russo-Ukrainian War was created as a result of territorial disputes between Russia and Ukraine, which could be traced back to the division of territory between the Russians and Ukrainians in ways that did not totally reflect the wishes of each ethnicity. The Israel-Palestine war traces its origins back to the original division of Mandatory Palestine between the Jewish State of Israel and Arab Palestinian Territories. However, after all the conflict, suffering, and division created as a result of the partitions discussed in this book, the long-term societal ramifications to the regions mentioned, as well as all other divided regions on Earth, tend to go under the radar.

Each region that is partitioned is split not only physically, but also linguistically, culturally, and religiously. After World War II, Poland lost its eastern third to the Soviet Union, who cleansed the Poles living in the area and repopulated it with Ukrainians, Belarusians, and Lithuanians. Although the Kresy, as this region was called, already had substantial populations of those minorities prior to the war, the region was by and large Polish and Roman Catholic. Cities like Wilno, Lwów, and Brześć were centers of Polish culture and language before the war, but the Soviets annexed them, removed the Poles living there (either through deportation or mass extermination), and repopulated them.

Fast forward to 1950, just five years after the war, and already the cities, renamed to Vilnius, Lviv, and Brest, were nearly cleared of any trace of Poland whatsoever. Assigned to Lithuania, Ukraine, and Belarus, respectively, these three cities and many others formerly in Poland saw their populations changed, places renamed, and entire character and culture overturned. In Ukraine or Belarus, Roman Catholic Poles were replaced with Orthodox Ukrainians and Belarusians, who followed a completely different form of Christianity. This is just one example of a partition that has had an apparent impact on the region socially, particularly because it is difficult to undo a partition. It is especially tough to undo one that has changed cultures and societies and one that happened a long time ago.

We've seen hostile nations like North and South Korea, whose geopolitical circumstances make reunification nearly impossible. Even nations that are amicable with each other, such as Ireland and Northern Ireland, have had trouble getting a unification movement going. Romania and Moldova were partitioned a very long time ago, but both are very friendly, both have retained similar cultures, and both have even openly discussed reunification. Even though all of these situations are different, all of them are very tough to navigate.

But what about the instances where, against the odds, a partition has been reversed? Take Germany, for example. After the Second World War, Germany was partitioned into a capitalist West and Communist East to be allied with NATO and the USSR, respectively. West Germany quickly recovered financially from the burden of World War II, becoming one of Europe's strongest economies despite being utterly destroyed. Many of its former monuments and structures were rebuilt, and those that weren't were replaced with new, sleek, modern edifices. East Germany, meanwhile, was left with a Communist,

Soviet-run economy that couldn't sustain a rebuild. They also had a government that was keen to wipe out any vestiges of the former German Empire or anything to do with monarchism and imperialism, as they viewed it. For example, the foundation of the Prussian Berlin Palace, caught in East Germany, was blown up by the communists and replaced with a public space, on which was eventually built the Palace of the Republic, a grandiose socialist building that housed the East's Parliament, as well as a shopping mall and ballroom, among other facilities. Other buildings that were ruined in the East were replaced with somewhat drab, boxy buildings typical of socialist nations at the time. Entire cities were rebuilt with huge, extremely basic apartments.

The German capital of Berlin was split between the two German nations, and the same architectural differences are present today, even though the nation is reunified and the West has invested trillions of dollars into bringing the East to its level. When I went to Germany in 2022, it was very clear which parts of Berlin were formerly West German and which were East. As a whole, East Germany still has some notable differences from the West. A 2018 study by the Pew Research Center placed the former West Germany's per capita GDP at €42,971 versus Eastern Germany's €32,108. Productivity in the East was, therefore, almost 75% of the West's. The dominant faith in the East, after years of Communist rule, has become atheism/irreligion, even though the territories that comprised East Germany were formerly almost entirely Lutheran.

It is clear that partitions have had permanent effects even on societies that were able to undo those divisions. This applies not only to partitions that happened recently or those that are extant; rather, any partition in history has had an impact on the surrounding area and, in some cases, the whole world. It is important that we recognize the true impact that partitions have had on the world, not only changing people, nations, and societies but also the entire world and our perception of and interactions with it.

Bibliography

Allcock, John B. and Lampe, John R.. "Yugoslavia." Encyclopedia Britannica, 27 Mar. 2024, https://www.britannica.com/place/Yugoslavia-former-federated-nation-1929-2003. Accessed 3 April 2024.

Aughey, Arthur H., Bottigheimer, Karl S., Jones, Emrys, Coulter, Colin and Smyth, Jim. "Northern Ireland." Encyclopedia Britannica, 2 Apr. 2024, https://www.britannica.com/place/Northern-Ireland. Accessed 3 April 2024.

Bakshi, G.D. "The War in Chechnya: A Military Analysis." *Strategic Analysis*, Columbia University, Aug. 2000, ciaotest.cc.columbia.edu/olj/sa/sa_aug00bag01.html. Accessed 30 Mar. 2024.

Bettmann. *Soldiers Walking Down Road. History.com*, assets.editorial.aetnd.com/uploads/2009/11/korean-war-gettyimages-514954082.jpg?width=2048&height=1024&crop=2048%3A1024%2Csmart&quality=75&auto=webp. Accessed 3 Apr. 2024.

Britannica, The Editors of Encyclopaedia. "Kim Il-Sung." Encyclopedia Britannica, 19 Mar. 2024, https://www.britannica.com/biography/Kim-Il-Sung. Accessed 3 April 2024.

Britannica, The Editors of Encyclopaedia. "collapse of the Soviet Union." Encyclopedia Britannica, 17 Feb. 2024, https://www.britannica.com/event/the-collapse-of-the-Soviet-Union. Accessed 30 March 2024.

CIA. *Israel*. 1988. *Library of Congress*, tile.loc.gov/image-services/iiif/service:gmd:gmd7:g7500:g7500:ct001575/full/pct:12.5/0/default.jpg. Accessed 3 Apr. 2024.

Clarke, Stephen. Ireland: New Arbitration Act. 2010. Web Page. Retrieved from the Library of Congress, <www.loc.gov/item/global-legal-monitor/2010-05-21/ireland-new-arbitration-act/>.

Conquest, Robert, McCauley, Martin, Pipes, Richard E. and Dewdney, John C.. "Soviet Union." Encyclopedia Britannica, 3 Apr. 2024, https://www.britannica.com/place/Soviet-Union. Accessed 3 April 2024.

Crawley, Aidan. *An anti-Brexit poster in Newry. The Irish Times*, www.irishtimes.com/resizer/-n3yGaKzM Y A D m 4 n V 9 r u 2 B T x 5 y g 8 = / 1 6 0 0 x 0 / filters:format(jpg):quality(70)/cloudfront-eu-

central-1.images.arcpublishing.com/irishtimes/
POJL3MP4SCNNHL4HQNTCI2Z2WA.jpg. Accessed
3 Apr. 2024.

dissolution of the Ottoman Empire. Encyclopaedia Britannica,
www.britannica.com/summary/Decline-of-the-
Ottoman-Empire#/media/1/434996/250828. Accessed
3 Apr. 2024.

Fanning, Ronan, Boland, Frederick Henry, Ranelagh,
John O'Beirne, Kay, Sean and Edwards, Robert Walter
Dudley. "Ireland." Encyclopedia Britannica, 3 Apr. 2024,
https://www.britannica.com/place/Ireland. Accessed 3
April 2024.

"File:Punch Congo Rubber Cartoon.Jpg." *Wikipedia,*
Wikimedia Foundation, commons.wikimedia.org/
wiki/File:Punch_congo_rubber_cartoon.jpg. Accessed
3 Apr. 2024.

Gandhi and Jinnah in Bombay. 1944. *PICRYL,* picryl.
com/media/gandhi-and-jinnah-in-bombay-5f912c.
Accessed 3 Apr. 2024.

Great Britain. Foreign Office. Historical Section. Partition
of Africa. London, H.M. Stationery off, 1920. Pdf.
Retrieved from the Library of Congress, <www.loc.
gov/item/a22000946/>.

Hahn, Bae-ho, Yu, Woo-ik, Lee, Chan, Lew, Young Ick and Lee, Jung Ha. "North Korea." Encyclopedia Britannica, 3 Apr. 2024, https://www.britannica.com/place/North-Korea. Accessed 3 April 2024.

Hamilton, Angus. Korea. New York, C. Scribner's sons, 1904. Pdf. Retrieved from the Library of Congress, <www.loc.gov/item/04024775/>.

Heitzman, James, Robert L Worden, and Library Of Congress. Federal Research Division. India: A Country Study. [Washington, D.C.: Federal Research Division, Library of Congress: For sale by the Supt. of Docs., U.S. G.P.O, 1996] Pdf. Retrieved from the Library of Congress, <www.loc.gov/item/96019266/>.

History.com Editors, editor. "Korean War." *History.com*, History, 11 May 2022, www.history.com/topics/asian-history/korean-war. Accessed 30 Mar. 2024.

---. "Korean War." *History.com*, HISTORY, 9 november 2009, www.history.com/topics/asian-history/korean-war. Accessed 3 Apr. 2024.

Kulik, Rebecca M.. "partition of India." Encyclopedia Britannica, 28 Mar. 2024, https://www.britannica.com/event/Partition-of-India. Accessed 30 March 2024.

Lee, Jung Ha, Lee, Kwang-rin, Lew, Young Ick, Lee, Ki-baik and Hahn, Bae-ho. "Korea." Encyclopedia Britannica, 29 Feb. 2024, https://www.britannica.com/place/Korea. Accessed 30 March 2024.

Milekic, Sven. *Josip Broz Tito (left) and Joseph Stalin. Balkan Insight*, BIRN, balkaninsight.com/2018/06/28/historic-tito-stalin-split-marked-in-croatia-06-28-2018/. Accessed 3 Apr. 2024.

Mitzelfelt, Brad, Sgt. *Persian Gulf War: machine gun*. 1991. *Encyclopaedia Britannica*, www.britannica.com/event/Persian-Gulf-War#/media/1/452778/162336. Accessed 3 Apr. 2024.

PALESTINIAN NEWS & INFORMATION AGENCY (WAFA) IN CONTRACT WITH APAIMAGES. Johns Hopkins University Hub, hub.jhu.edu/2023/10/20/humanitarian-health-effects-of-israel-hamas-war/. Accessed 3 Apr. 2024.

Partition_of_India_1947. 11 Feb. 2017. *Wikimedia Commons*, Wikimedia, 5 July 2017, upload.wikimedia. org/wikipedia/commons/3/3b/Partition_of_India_1947_en.svg. Accessed 3 Apr. 2024.

Ray, Michael. "Why Did the Soviet Union Collapse?." Encyclopedia Britannica, 25 Aug. 2023, https://www.

britannica.com/story/why-did-the-soviet-union-collapse. Accessed 30 March 2024.

"Scramble-for-Africa-1880-1913." 21 July 2020. *Wikimedia Commons*, Wikimedia, 21 July 2020, en.m.wikipedia.org/wiki/File:Scramble-for-Africa-1880-1913-v2.png. Accessed 3 Apr. 2024.

Socialist Federal Republic of Yugoslavia as of January 1991. United Nations | International Residual Mechanism for Criminal Tribunals, United Nations, www.icty.org/x/image/ABOUTimagery/Yugoslavia%20maps/3_%20yugoslavia_map_1991_sml_en.png. Accessed 3 Apr. 2024.

Thatcher, Jonathan. "United Korea economy could pass Japan: Goldman Sachs." Reuters [London], 21 Sept. 2009. Reuters, www.reuters.com/article/idUSTRE58K0OA/. Accessed 8 Apr. 2024.

This map shows how the conflict surged back and forth. The truce line added 850 square miles to North Korea below the 38th parallel, 2,350 square miles to South Korea above it. *Britannica Kids*, Encyclopaedia Britannica, kids.britannica.com/students/assembly/view/54581. Accessed 3 Apr. 2024.

United States Central Intelligence Agency. Soviet Union administrative divisions. [Washington, D.C.:

Central Intelligence Agency, 1983] Map. Retrieved from the Library of Congress, <www.loc.gov/item/2005626378/>.

United States Central Intelligence Agency. United Kingdom, Northern Ireland. [Washington, D.C.: Central Intelligence Agency, 1987] Map. Retrieved from the Library of Congress, <www.loc.gov/item/89693217/>.

Vaughan, Don. "Why Is Ireland Two Countries?." Encyclopedia Britannica, 11 Feb. 2020, https://www.britannica.com/story/why-is-ireland-two-countries. Accessed 30 March 2024.

Vyatkin, Vladimir. *Mikhail Gorbachev, 1987. Encyclopaedia Britannica*, www.britannica.com/biography/Mikhail-Gorbachev#/media/1/238982/235089. Accessed 3 Apr. 2024.

Webster, Richard A., Magdoff, Harry and Nowell, Charles E.. "Western colonialism." Encyclopedia Britannica, 18 Dec. 2023, https://www.britannica.com/topic/Western-colonialism. Accessed 30 March 2024.

Wolpert, Stanley A., Calkins, Philip B., Schwartzberg, Joseph E., Alam, Muzaffar, Thapar, Romila, Champakalakshmi, R., Dikshit, K.R., Allchin, Frank

Raymond, Spear, T.G. Percival, Subrahmanyam, Sanjay, Srivastava, A.L. and Raikar, Sanat Pai. "India." Encyclopedia Britannica, 3 Apr. 2024, https://www.britannica.com/place/India. Accessed 3 April 2024.

Yu, Woo-ik, Lee, Chan, Im, Hyug-Baeg, Hahn, Bae-ho and Lew, Young Ick. "South Korea." Encyclopedia Britannica, 3 Apr. 2024, https://www.britannica.com/place/South-Korea. Accessed 3 April 2024.

Ziring, Lawrence and Burki, Shahid Javed. "Pakistan." Encyclopedia Britannica, 1 Apr. 2024, https://www.britannica.com/place/Pakistan. Accessed 3 April 2024.

Agastya *is a writer, blogger, debater, and the founder of "Youth for Sustainable Future," a nonprofit dedicated to promoting global sustainability. He's had a passionate interest in history and international affairs since elementary school. A two-time gold medalist at the International History Olympiad and 2022 International History Bowl Champion, he keenly follows global events and politics. In his free time, he enjoys traveling, reading books, watching movies, and playing the piano. He lives in Long Island, New York, with his parents and his little sister.*